PLANTS & GARDENS

BROOKLYN BOTANIC GARDEN RECORD

ANNUALS
A GARDENER'S GUIDE

1992

Plants & Gardens, Brooklyn Botanic Garden Record (ISSN 0362-5850)

is published quarterly at 1000 Washington Ave., Brooklyn, N.Y. 11225, by the **Brooklyn Botanic Garden, Inc.**

Subscription included in Botanic Garden membership dues ($25.00 per year).

ISBN # 0-945352-76-X

Brooklyn Botanic Garden

STAFF FOR THIS EDITION:

ROB PROCTOR, GUEST EDITOR

BARBARA B. PESCH, DIRECTOR OF PUBLICATIONS

JANET MARINELLI, EDITOR

AND THE EDITORIAL COMMITTEE OF THE BROOKLYN BOTANIC GARDEN

BEKKA LINDSTROM, ART DIRECTOR

JUDITH D. ZUK, PRESIDENT, BROOKLYN BOTANIC GARDEN

ELIZABETH SCHOLTZ, DIRECTOR EMERITUS, BROOKLYN BOTANIC GARDEN

STEPHEN K-M. TIM, VICE PRESIDENT, SCIENCE & PUBLICATIONS

COVER: PHOTOGRAPHY BY ROB PROCTOR

PLANTS & GARDENS
BROOKLYN BOTANIC GARDEN RECORD

ANNUALS
A GARDENER'S GUIDE

VOL. 48, No. 4, WINTER 1992

HANDBOOK #133

Illustrations by Jill Buck

Stock, *Matthiola incana*, adds a stately presence to the garden, scents the air, attracts butterflies and is a good cut flower.

FOREWORD

The resurgence of interest in annuals may have something to do with fashion. They go in and out of fashion every generation or so. Annuals enjoyed their heyday during the Victorian era, when the new bedding plants had a virtual monopoly in the most fashionable, formal gardens.

The reawakened interest may also be attributed to the popularity of the cottage garden style. Lush, overstuffed and slightly madcap, cottage gardens have inspired garden tastemakers ever since the waning of the Victorian bedding craze, when gardens took on a less structured, more naturalistic look. Many gardeners have taken an interest in the old-fashioned flowers they remember from their grandparents' gardens.

ROB PROCTOR *is the author of the Antique Flower series:* Perennials *(HarperCollins, 1990),* Annuals *(1991), and* Country Flowers *(1991) as well as the forthcoming* The Potted Bulb: Volumes I and II *(Simon and Schuster, 1993.) He teaches, paints and gardens in Denver, Colorado.*

Perhaps we value annuals again because of their beauty and grace and the form of their flowers and foliage. Many annuals have a stately presence and flower freely, recommending them for a place in beds and borders in sun and shade. They climb and trail, decorate patios and porches and sit on the breakfast table as cut flowers. They scent the air, spice up the salad and screen the compost pile.

Wherever gardeners live, annuals play an important role. Some thrive in a sultry summer, others bloom in northern latitudes and mountainous regions. Some are so adaptable that they find a home in gardens throughout the continent.

Besides their beauty, dependability and ease of culture, annuals — in their amazing diversity — present a gardener with a multitude of options each year. Some are a passing fancy, while others earn a permanent place in the border and in the heart. Perhaps annuals have come back into fashion for good.

ROB PROCTOR
Guest Editor

THE VICTORIAN LEGACY

BY MARY FORSELL

Amaranthus caudatus

The Victorian era was an exuberant, even dizzying time. It gave us the telegraph, the double-decker bus, the skyscraper and endless other inventions; introduced a pastiche of pastimes, from Bingo to badminton; and gave rise to such diverse institutions as the beauty contest and the Daughters of the American Revolution. But of greatest interest to gardeners is the development of the greenhouse and the subsequent obsession with carpet bedding. Often breathtaking, sometimes garish but always inventive, carpet bedding is one of the most eccentric and fascinating styles in garden history.

The events that would eventually lead to the carpet bedding craze, which relied heavily on annuals for its effects, began in the 1820s and gained momentum on into the 30s. Prominent English garden writer John Claudius Loudon was leading an impassioned crusade against the estab-

MARY FORSELL *is the author of* Heirloom Herbs *(Villard, 1991) and* Berries *(Bantam, 1989). The Herbal Grove will be published by Villard in winter 1994. She gardens in Spring Lake, New Jersey.*

Left: Dusty miller, *Senecio cineraria,* was popular in Victorian carpet beds. Here it is interwoven with marigolds.

7

lished English landscape garden (a style, incidentally, that had been developed to counter the extreme formalism of European gardens). Loudon criticized the idea of creating a garden that merely copied nature's grandeur, believing that it was deceptive to the viewer. It was much more honest, and tasteful, felt Loudon, to create a garden filled with exotic plants — species that couldn't possibly have grown naturally in the landscape — and arrange them in such a manner as to show distinctly the human hand at work.

Loudon's philosophy was well timed. The Victorian era was a period of intense plant exploration. European and North American plant hunters visited jungles, rain forests and other remote locations in the southern hemisphere in search of species whose novel shapes and colors might win them a place in gardens back home. Horticulturists experimented with hybridization on an unprecedented scale. The new, improved greenhouse, made pos-

sible by technological advances of the Industrial Revolution, was fully exploited to house this influx of exotic foreigners.

In the first half of the century, English estate gardeners created the bedding system, a technique for displaying exotics in seasonally changing vignettes designed to bedazzle onlookers, much like modern-day department store windows. The plants were sometimes of one type planted *en masse* by the thousands; other times, several different kinds were contrasted.

These garden design currents swiftly took hold among the genteel of America, and soon colorful beds became standard on their pleasure grounds. With the election of Andrew Jackson to the presidency in 1828, began the reign of the common man. "Old Hickory," as Jackson was known, encouraged greater participation of the general populace in government, imparting a sense of entitlement to the middle class. Like the wealthy land barons, the middle classes adopted the practice of exotic bed-

In their bedding schemes, the Victorians often planted one type of annual *en masse*. Zinnias were favorites, especially the low-growing forms.

In flowerbeds along the walkway to the house, Victorians strove to proclaim that they were people of style and taste. Here, pink ivy geraniums and spider flowers combine handsomely with plants grown for their gray foliage.

ding to proclaim that they were people of taste and substance. Of course, this required a greenhouse, which made this garden structure a coveted feature of the middle-class home.

The nineteenth century in general was a period of intense style consciousness, and as the decades progressed, this fervor only grew. International exhibitions were especially important in disseminating fashion and stimulating an appetite for the exotic. The Crystal Palace, the ultimate greenhouse, was designed by Joseph Paxton and erected in London in 1851 to host the exhibition titled "The Industry of All Nations." International exhibitions followed in quick succession, including the 1876 Centennial Celebration in Philadelphia.

The era also saw the rise of many architectural revival styles. In America, wealthy industry barons constructed grand estates in the French Renaissance chateau and Italian Villa styles. Undaunted, the burgeoning middle class created its own home castles in the Queen Anne and Greek Revival modes, among others. Not known for their minimalism, such homes were filled with imported porcelain, exotic carpets and cabinets bursting with curios, sculpture, beadwork and oversize floral arrangements. Mass production allowed everyone — not just the very rich — to bedeck their homes with all manner of machine-made furniture and frippery. Home decorating magazines sprang up to advise people on how to design their

Phlox drummondii, dwarf phlox, was often combined with other low, clipped annuals to form "knots" reminiscent of the parterre designs of previous eras.

homes, and never had so many exotic choices been available. As Russell Lynes wrote in his book *The Taste-Makers*, it was at mid-century that E. B. Bigelow invented a power loom "to make Brussels and tapestry carpets, which were eventually to cover the floors of America with flora and fauna in colors that sang at the tops of their lungs."

A popular home decorating publication of the day, *Appleton's Journal*, reported in its 1887 "Editor's Table" that "color and . . . splendor" were decidedly back in vogue and declared that the "delight in form, and light and shadow, and pomp, has come back to us — with many modifications, of course, but with much of its old sense of beauty for beauty's sake."

How aptly these words can be applied to concurrent movements in gardening. By the late Victorian period (which began around 1870), head gardeners of the British gentry, still the leaders in horticultural exploits, attempted to outdo one another in intricate arrangements of plants. Instead of merely displaying mass groupings of exotics on their lawns, these gardeners began to create intricate and challenging patterns that relied on strong color contrasts.

America caught wind of this horticultural development, and carpet bedding (as the technique came to be known) became the rage everywhere. It was the quintessential example of "beauty for beauty's sake" and the perfect complement to the exuberant architecture and interior design of the day. Carpet bedding involved using primarily low-growing flowers and foliage plants to create fantastically intricate patterns. So that not a detail could go by unnoticed, such beds were often angled slightly. Gardens were also positioned to be admired from second-story porches or bay windows. Although perennials were also used in carpet-bedding schemes, annuals were of special appeal to the Victorians as by their nature they provided continuous and profuse bloom and allowed for greater experimentation. Some designs were simple spirals or wavy bands of annuals, often in violent juxtapositions of color, consisting of scarlet sage (*Salvia splendens*), flaming yellow or red Flora's paintbrush (*Emilia coccinea*, then known as *Cacalia*), crimson pheasant's eye (*Adonis annua*), blue cornflower (*Centaurea cyanus*), yellow dwarf zinnia (*Zinnia elegans*), insistently orange African daisy (*Arctotis breviscapa*) and eye-catching pink rose of heaven (*Lychnis coelirosa*). Concentric rings of different flowers, building progressively in height, might be punctuated at the center with a tall, focal point such as love-lies-bleeding (*Amaranthus caudatus*), prickly poppy (*Argemone grandiflora*), spider flower (*Cleome hassleriana*) or the towering castor-oil plant (*Ricinus communis*), cultivated for its foliage, either growing out of the ground or from a decorative urn.

There were also carpet beds reminiscent of parterre designs of previous eras, with "knots" of low, clipped, interwoven annuals. Dusty miller (*Senecio cineraria*), floss flower (*Ageratum houstonianum*), dwarf annual phlox (*Phlox drummondii*), dwarf Mexican marigold (*Tagetes tenuifolia* var. *erinus*), stonecrop (*Sedum caeruleum*) and rose moss (*Portulaca grandiflora*) were suitable choices for such beds.

On the more stylized end, carpet bedders applied their art to create all manner of figures: birds, crosses, coats of arms, shields, letters, trefoils, human forms, urns, stars, fish — anything that could be "drawn" with flowers and foliage. Popular foliage plants for these categories were coleus (*Coleus* x *blumei*), with crimson and green frilled leaves, and fancy-leaved geranium (*Pelargonium* spp.), with beautiful foliage rippled with gold, ivory, scarlet and green. Complementing the foliage were profusely flowering candytuft (annual *Iberis* species), China pink (*Dianthus chinensis*), pot marigold (*Calendula officinalis*), forget-me-not (annual *Myosotis* species), baby blue eyes (*Nemophila menziesii*) and mignonette (*Reseda odorata*).

Today, echoes of this lavish style can usually be found only in public places: flower beds spelling out a town's name on a grassy knoll, theme parks intermingling freakish topiary with whirling displays of lollipop-colored annuals. By and large, most home gardeners opt for more subdued (some would say "bland") approaches. How exciting it must have been to live in an era that encouraged such outlandish gardening escapades! Carpet bedding was a pure expression of Victorian *joie de vivre*, a sentiment that spilled over into everything they did. Witness a bulletin entitled "Annual Flowers," by G. N. Lauman and L. H. Bailey, published by the Cornell University Agriculture Experiment Station in January 1899. The authors describe 459 annuals in lists with characteristic Victorian enthusiasm: "These lists emphasize the riches which are now at the disposal of every homemaker, and which the enterprising seedsmen have brought from the ends of the earth." The Victorians were well aware of both the old stock of classic annuals and the horticultural gems newly available to them. Like jewelers, they combined and displayed these gems in the most spectacular settings possible.

ANNUALS FOR THE MIXED BORDER

BY LAUREN SPRINGER

Alcea rosea

Too often, annuals are grown apart from the rest of the garden in segregated beds, instead of being allowed to mingle and socialize with perennials and shrubs. The most popular cultivars are bred for ever more outlandish flower size and color, making it all the more difficult to integrate them effectively with the more subtle plants that make up a garden.

LAUREN SPRINGER, *who gardens in northern Colorado, writes a weekly gardening column for* The Denver Post.

Left: Annuals mingle with perennials in a lush, colorful flower border.

Fortunately, a number of old-fashioned and less familiar annuals can still be called upon to do double duty in the mixed border, lengthening the floral display, filling gaps, adding fragrance, color, form and texture. Unlike their overbred, gaudy cousins, these plants don't overpower their neighbors; they enhance them. They have retained their original grace: some semblance of balance between leaf, stem and flower remains. Many are fragrant; many thrive in less-than-optimal soil and water conditions. Best of all, a number of them self-sow, a delightful quality that relieves the gardener of yearly seeding and adds a degree of spontaneity to a planting that is impossible to replicate.

Some dependable self sowers are large enough that they require that you reserve space for them: bulky-leaved borage (*Borago officinalis*) with starry blue flowers that enhance both pastels and the warmer reds, yellows and oranges, for example, or bronze fennel (*Foeniculum vulgare* 'Pur-

pureum'), a three- to four-foot tender perennial with feathery, anise-scented foliage . 'Italian White' sunflower, quite dwarf compared to its coarser relative, must still be allowed a good four by four feet if its distinctive, chocolate-eyed pale yellow flower heads are not to be cramped. *Hibiscus trionum*, with the same beautiful flower color, needs a bit less room. Each creamy blossom stays open only a few hours a day, but so many are produced as long as the weather remains warm that you don't notice these fleeting comings and goings. It goes by the pretty name "flower of the hour." Old-fashioned *Cosmos bipinnatus* can rival a shrub in girth when its ferny foliage has reached midsummer proportions. The newer cultivar 'Sonata' grows to a more manageable two feet, but I have yet to see whether its progeny retain this smaller stature.

The self-sowing annuals more easily allowed to run rampant in the garden are those smaller, narrower ones with sparse

Many old-fashioned annuals can lengthen the floral display and add fragrance, color, form and texture to a perennial border.

foliage that slip in and out of other plants without usurping precious space. A rose garden is much improved by allowing sweet alyssum (*Lobularia maritima*) to carpet the base of the shrubs. The white, soft lavender and rose colors complement the tones of old garden roses. For the brighter orange, scarlet and yellow hybrid teas and floribundas, sky-blue annuals love-in-a-mist (*Nigella damascena*) or Chinese forget-me-not (*Cynoglossum amabile*) make an effective foil. Tall spikes of larkspur (*Consolida ambigua*), the lazy gardener's delphinium, contrast with the rounded form of the rose blossoms. A haze of purple *Verbena bonariensis* (*V. patagonica*) among late-season flushes of pink, white and butter-yellow floribundas brings the rose season to a lovely close.

In drier, less fertile soil, hot pink annual catchfly (*Silene armeria*) mixes with pastels or, for the more daring colorist, with gold- and orange-flowered perennials and annuals. Drought-tolerant annuals in sunshine colors such as tulip poppy (*Hunnemannia fumariifolia*), California poppy (*Eschscholzia californica*), tiny Dahlberg daisy (*Dyssodia tenuiloba*) and blazing star (*Mentzelia lindleyi*) are all fine-textured enough to mix in a fiesta-colored jamboree with the catchfly without becoming garish. If you can't stomach such a color combination, try pristine white prickly poppy (*Argemone platyceras*) with lovely, silver-veined bluish foliage, and jewels-of-Opar, (*Talinum crassifolium*) with airy sprays of rose flowers and peach-colored seeds. The ruby-red, diaphanous flowers of annual flax (*Linum grandiflorum* 'Rubrum') are gorgeous combined with deep, true-blue *Delphinium chinensis*, an easy annual that also self-sows prolifically. And for mauve, lavender and powder-pink tones, opium poppies (*Papaver somniferum*) with their tissue-paper petals and the newer 'Fairy Wings' or 'Mother of Pearl' poppies are ideal.

Tall spikes of larkspur (*Consolida ambigua*) can substitute for delphinium in the border.

Old-fashioned annuals are once again chic, thanks to the renewed interest in heirloom plants and cottage gardening. It is wonderful to be able to find seed of plants that for decades had only been available from generous gardeners willing to pass seeds and seedlings over the fence. For those of us surrounded by a sea of suburban lawns, the satiny flowers of *Clarkia amoena*, the fragrant, tiered, rose-pink blossoms of lemon balm (*Monarda citriodora*), flaxlike, fuschia-colored corn-cockle (*Agrostemma githago*) and similar *Lychnis coeli-rosa* and the daintily veined pink petals of *Malva sylvestris* were coveted but rarely obtainable. Now it is much easier to find seed or transplants, and these graceful flowers can be tucked among the perennials of summer or in the spaces left by tulips and daffodils.

A group of annuals indispensable for the perennial border, especially the young one in which plants have not yet matured and there is too much soil to be seen, are the annual weavers. These petite plants sprawl and trail, threading themselves between the more substantial members of a border. Campanulalike white and purple cup flower (*Nierembergia hippomanica*), the blue- and pink-flowered viper's bugloss (*Echium lycopsis*), lavender and white thread-leaf verbena (*Glandularia tenuisecta*, syn. *Verbena tenuisecta*) and the shrimp-pink jester-cap flowered *Diascia* spp. all do well in infertile soil with little water. Two delicate daisies are also well-suited to these conditions: Swan River daisy (*Brachycome iberidifolia*), in shades of lavender, purple and white, and Mexican fleabane (*Erigeron karvinskianus*), pink in bud and white in flower. There is even a toned-down version of the garish marigold ideal for weaving — the 'Little Gem' series, including 'Lemon Gem' and 'Tangerine Gem', with tiny single flowers borne for months on end.

Quite the opposite of the weavers are the showier annuals whose flowers rival the newest hybrid petunia or zinnia in size and color but whose more graceful growth habits enable them to blend easily into existing plantings. Shrublike *Lavatera trimestris*, with huge pink and white mallow blossoms and attractive maplelike foliage, can rival any perennial in the border. Pale pink hawksbeard (*Crepis rubra*), the deep crimson, ball-shaped plumed thistle (*Cirsium japonicum*) or the brilliant yellow, orange or red pendulous tassel flower (*Emilia coccinea*) all jazz up a planting without becoming overbearing. Gentian blue *Salvia patens* is the perfect companion to fiery tassel flower. Many salvias and their close relatives the agastaches, annual in cold climates, have showy, brilliantly colored flowers yet retain a sinewy form that the stubby, more common annuals lack.

Tall pink *Dahlia merckii*, perennial in warmer climates, has none of the girth and need for staking that the large "dinner plate" hybrids have. Yet it is stately and imposing

LAUREN SPRINGER

Marigolds, salvia, dahlias and ornamental peppers comprise the hot-colored flower walk at Longwood Gardens.

towards the back of the border with pink and white *Cleome hassleriana*. Annual black-eyed Susan (*Rudbeckia hirta*) is another lovely and dependable old stand-by.

Foliage is not usually an annual's strong suit, but several tender perennials and biennials can add this element to a mixed border. Giant cardoon (*Cynara cardunculus*), a tender perennial closely related to the artichoke, has pewter foliage that is striking with both hot and cool colors, as are the equally large yet whiter leaves of biennial Scottish thistle (*Onopordum acanthium*). Both these members of the thistle family send up flowers their second year in the garden, but the foliage is what makes them worth growing. Smaller *Cirsium spinosissimum* is better where space is at a premium: the viciously spiny foliage is gray-green edged and marbled with white. In flower, the plant loses all its charm, so it should be grown as an annual for its first-year foliage rosette. Woolly white mullein leaves (*Verbascum bombyciferum*) remain a low rosette the first year, sending up a tall, attractive yellow-flowered spike the second year; this drastic change in stature makes them a bit hard to place in the garden. Horned poppy (*Glaucium* spp.) grows scalloped blue-gray leaves which it tops with honey-colored flowers its second year. All these biennials can grow in meager soil with little water but require full sun. For the most striking, richly hued, glossy maroon foliage, try *Dahlia* 'Bishop of Llandaff', with scarlet flowers that are set off perfectly by the foliage. It adds a smoldering, deep tone, but use it only in a well-watered and fed border.

Finally, several biennials can provide the much-needed vertical element to the often overly rounded, "lumpy-lump" border. Old-fashioned foxgloves (*Digitalis purpurea*) lend a fairytale quality to a partly shaded area. Poison hemlock (*Conium maculatum*) is lovely in leaf and flower, but should not be

Lobularia maritima, sweet alyssum, and vibrant red cockscomb, *Celosia cristata*.

used where there are children or animals. Its ferny foliage and lacy white flower umbels are taller than most gardeners and can soften the back of a border or a planting of shrubs. Queen Anne's lace, a close but edible relative, is more manageable at two to three feet. In full sun, the vibrancy of fiery orange-red standing cypress (*Ipomopsis rubra*) and the quaint charm of hollyhocks (*Alcea rosea*) are hard to match. On the shorter side, opalescent clary sage (*Salvia sclarea*), with great hairy gray-green leaves and a crisp, pungent fragrance, blends into just about any perennial border.

Annuals have long been pariahs among the horticultural tastemakers, and not without reason, as those most commonly seen are so limited in use. Aside from beds and containers, they have little place in the garden. The key is to look beyond those dozen or so plants at the wondrous assortment of annuals that complement the more permanent members of the garden.

DISCOVERING NATIVE ANNUALS

BY STEVEN FOSTER

Eschscholzia californica

olumbus left the Canary Islands in his three famous ships on September 5, 1492, making landfall a few weeks later. Few events in human history have had such a dramatic impact on the world, especially the plant world. Columbus's arrival ushered in a new era in plant distribution — worldwide, transoceanic distribution of plants through human intervention.

Writing about native annuals 500 years later, one is tempted to broaden the definition of "natives" to include Latin America. After all, South America has given us some of our best annuals: the brilliant trumpets of marvel of Peru (*Mirabilis jalapa*), the sweet-scented ornamental jasmine tobacco (*Nicotiana alata*) and the common nasturtium (*Tropaeolum majus*). As tempting as it is to include South American annual natives, we will narrow the definition of "native."

STEVEN FOSTER *is the author of* Echinacea: Nature's Immune Enhancer *(Healing Arts Press, 1991) and* Herbal Bounty *(Gibbs Smith, 1983) and co-author of* Herbal Emissaries: Bringing Chinese Herbs to the West *(Healing Arts Press, 1992) and* A Field Guide to Medicinal Plants: Eastern and Central North America *(Houghton Mifflin, 1990). He lives in Arkansas.*

Left: *Euphorbia marginata*, snow-on-the-mountain, a native of the Great Plains.

"Annuals" and "natives" have both become catchwords that require some definition. In some quarters annuals have become associated with the gardening klutz, the person who wants effortless results — instant color, instant satisfaction, something you can buy in six packs with blooms already in place. Annuals do lend themselves to horticultural mass marketing; the positive side of this is that they bring gardening to the non-gardener. Growing annuals from seed requires a little more effort, but still involves little more than putting the seeds in the ground and adding appropriate doses of water. Annuals are also excellent subjects for the horticultural experimenter. Beyond the plants available at the local nursery, or even the local supermarket, annuals offer endless possibilities for exploration and discovery.

The term "annuals" is more easily defined than the term "natives." Strictly speaking, to define a native plant, one must first establish the natural geographic boundaries of the species. Biologically speaking, if you grow a plant in its natural range, it is native. Outside those boundaries it is non-native. But it's not quite as simple as that. To use an analogy, although my ancestors were European transplants naturalized to the North American continent, I am a native of North America or, more precisely, a native of Maine. But in my chosen home of Arkansas, I will always be an alien. Is a California poppy still a native plant when grown in Maine? Not biologically speaking, but if you want to call it an "American native," then you are safe. What constitutes a native plant is relative to the area delineated in the conversation.

An annual technically is defined as a plant that completes its life cycle, from germination to maturity to death, in one growing season. Sometimes a plant is an "annual" by circumstance, such as the climate in which it is grown. Although perennial in its

Collinsia heterophylla, innocence, native to the western states.

native haunts, a plant may be annual when grown elsewhere. I grew sweet marjoram (*Origanum majorana*) in Maine for several years, believing it was an annual. Then I moved to California and was surprised to learn that the plant is a perennial. The same is true of the California poppy (*Eschscholzia californica*), California's state flower. In California or other parts of the country where the temperature does not dip below 0° F, it behaves as a short-lived perennial. But for most of North America, the California poppy is an annual. You could call it native to Arizona, Nevada, New Mexico, Oregon, Washington, Texas and, of course, California, but it is as alien to Maine as I am to Arkansas. Nevertheless, it has gained the attention of gardeners

Phacelia campanularia, California bluebells, also a western native, produces a delicate explosion of blue in the garden when planted *en masse*.

throughout the country as one of the most appreciated "native annuals." The feathery, dissected, blue-tinted leaves are like lace decorating the lustrous, bold, orange-gold, four-petaled blooms, which unfold in their brilliant splendor on sunny days, closing at night or under cloud cover.

E. californica is a highly variable species, which has at one time or another spawned over 100 descriptions and names. Now, however, it is recognized as a single, highly variable taxon. This variability produced varieties sporting gold-bronze, yellow, orange, orange-red, cream-white and rose-pink flowers. The delicate blooms, sometimes double, are up to three inches across. The plant grows from six to 18 inches in height.

The genus *Eschscholzia* was named for J.F. Eschscholtz (1793-1831), an Estonian explorer, biologist and physician. Once consisting of as many as 123 species, the genus is now recognized as possessing eight to ten species native to western North America. Specimens reached Europe as early as the 1790's and quickly became popular. The plant is now naturalized in at least a dozen countries of western and central Europe.

The plant is easy to grow, thriving in poor, sandy soil in full sun. If the soil is too rich, it will produce an abundance of vegetative growth with fewer blooms. Plant seeds about one-eighth inch deep after danger of frost has passed in spring. They germinate in about two weeks. Plant it directly in the garden, because California poppy does not transplant well.

The California poppy makes a good annual for the herb garden, adding color and the opportunity to appreciate its historical lore. The Costanoan Indians of central California placed one or two flower petals under a child's bed to induce sleep. A flower decoction was rubbed in the hair to kill lice. Indians of Mendocino County used an extract or wash of the fresh roots to allay toothache. The root's stupefying effects were said to have been utilized by native Americans who were gambling, presumably to dull the competition. The plant was chemically investigated as early as 1844. Nineteenth-century physicians found that an alcohol extract at a prescribed dose produced calm sleep while quieting pain.

While the California poppy is the best native annual that the state has contributed to horticulture, there are others. Take *Phacelia*, or California bluebells, a genus of about 150 species of the water-leaf family (Hydrophyllaceae), also native to a number of other western states, Mexico and the Andes. *P. campanularia* is bell-like in appearance as the species name implies. In *The English Flower Garden*, William Robinson called it "the best kind [of plant], free in its fine dark-blue flowers spotted with white in the throat; they last a long while, and the plant makes a pretty carpet in sunny places"; which brings me to their their use — mass planting. Although an individual *Phacelia* is less than riveting, planted *en masse* they produce a delicate explosion of blue in the garden.

Adapted to sandy, well-drained, poor soils, they thrive in full sun. Plant seeds in a cool spring soil after the last frost, tamping them lightly into the surface. Flowers bloom from mid-spring to mid-summer, depending upon the region. Other popular species include *P. tanacetifolia*, which grows from one to three feet tall and has leaves resembling those of tansy (*Tanacetum*). Phacelias reached Europe, and hence horticulture, in the 1830's. *Phacelia* also makes a good addition to the herb garden for color and historical value. The roots were used by various Indian groups of the western United States as a treatment for coughs and colds as well as stomach problems.

Collinsia, a genus in the figwort family (Scrophulariaceae) with about twenty species primarily from the western states, was introduced into English horticulture soon after its discovery by the Scottish botanist David Douglas (1798-1834). Named for Zaccheus Collins, botanist and former vice president of the Academy of Natural Sciences of Philadelphia, collinsias are popularly known as Chinese houses because the tiered whorls of flowers have a pagodalike appearance. Ranging from white, rose and lilac to bright blue, these plants deserve greater appreciation.

The most widely grown species, also called innocence, *C. heterophylla* (*C. bicolor*), has blue-lavender flowers with white markings. It grows from one to two feet tall, preferring a relatively moist, well-drained, rich soil and light shade. Given enough moisture, it will tolerate full sun. Sow seeds in late autumn or early spring, scratching them into the soil to a depth of about one-eighth inch. For the open-minded herb gardener, this is another opportunity to add color and historical appreciation. *C. parviflora* was used by the Navaho to make a horse run fast. The Natchez used the root of the eastern North American native *C. violacea* as a remedy for colds, coughs, consumption and whooping cough.

California and the Southwest in general have given us more annuals than any other region of the country. The arid regions of the West explode in color in the spring as dozens of annual species go through their entire life cycles, from the sprouting of

Native to the Great Plains and surrounding regions, *Coreopsis tinctoria*, plains coreopsis, blooms freely in almost any garden soil.

seed to seed dispersal, in six weeks or less. It is only for a short period that the conditions are right for lush growth in America's dry regions. Eastward-ranging species also provide interesting — though fewer — native annuals for the flower garden.

Native to the Great Plains and adjacent regions, plains coreopsis, plains tickseed or calliopsis (*Coreopsis tinctoria*) has been a popular addition to seed mixes in recent years. It has escaped from cultivation and irregularly established itself in the Southeast. Sporting seven to eight yellow-orange, triangular ray flowers, usually reddish brown at the base, this glabrous annual is a familiar sight along roadsides of the prairies, blooming from June through August.

The plant is sometimes traded as "Calliopsis," which is an obsolete generic name once applied to showy annuals separated from the genus *Coreopsis*. Calliopsis is derived from the Greek *kallistos* (beautiful) and *opsis* (eye), referring to the attractive, reddish-centered blooms. *C. tinctoria* was once known as *Calliopsis elegans* in the garden trade. Coreopsis comes from the Greek *koris* (bug) and *opsis* (translated to mean "resemblance" in this case), referring to the buglike appearance of the fruits. The ticklike seeds also give rise to the common name tickseed.

C. tinctoria is a hardy, showy annual that can be raised with little care, blooming freely in almost any garden soil. In its native haunts it seems to prefer seasonally

damp, disturbed sites such as sandy ditches or low sandy ground. Growing to about three feet in height, it is best planted in the middle or back of a seasonal border. Sow seeds in early spring, covering them with about one-quarter inch of soil. It is an excellent annual for cut flowers or naturalizing in semiwild areas.

Few native annuals are grown more for their foliage than their flower, but this is the case with snow-on-the-mountain (*Euphorbia marginata*). Actually, the leaflike bracts extending beyond the flowers are the showy part of this plant. Often cultivated, it has frequently escaped and become more common in its native Great Plains since human settlement. This member of the spurge family grows from one to three feet in height. Usually unbranched, the broken stems exude milky latex, typical of spurge family members.

The bracts, sometimes entirely white or variegated, are most prominent in June through October. Native from Minnesota to Texas and Montana to New Mexico, it prefers limy prairies, roadsides, pastures and wastelands. In the garden it is easy to grow from seed, which can be sown in spring or fall at a depth of about one-eighth to one-fourth inch. Given a sunny location, it doesn't seem to be too particular about soils. The plant is not suitable for cut flower arrangements because the milky latex can be highly caustic and can cause dermatitis. It has even been used to brand cattle.

These are a few native American annuals that have found their way into horticulture. Some, like the California poppy, had only to be seen once to be introduced into the trade. Others, such as *Collinsia*, needed a champion — someone like David Douglas — to promote them. Many more native annuals await discovery by gardeners. Columbus, after all, didn't really "discover" America, he was simply the first to promote its development.

Phacelia tanacetifolia, which grows from one to three feet tall, is honey-scented and a favorite of bees.

In Search of
Antique Annuals

by Marilyn Barlow

Ipomoea alba

Flowers — they are made solely to gladden the heart of man, for a light to his eyes, for a living inspiration of grace to his spirit, for a perpetual admiration." So elegant and florid, the quote comes from the Victorian era seed catalogue of Comstock, Ferre & Co.

Many of the flowers that captured the hearts and souls of gardeners back then are still in favor today, morning glories, bachelor buttons and nasturtiums among them.

Seed merchant Marilyn Barlow *specializes in antique and heirloom varieties. Her mail order company, Select Seeds, is based in Union, Connecticut.*

Others have quietly disappeared from gardens and are rarely found in seed catalogues: flowers with nostalgic names such as 'Painted Lady' sweet pea (*Lathyrus odoratus*), double carnation-flowered poppy (*Papaver somniferum*), azure-blue single 'Emperor William' cornflower (*Centaurea cyanus*) and sweetly-scented white marvel of Peru (*Mirabilis longiflora*). Still others, endangered or perhaps lost, may survive only in print in the lists and descriptions of seed catalogs of the past.

Within the aged covers of these catalogs one finds a celebration of diversity. The Burpee's *Farm Annual* of 1903 lists over 600 annual flower varieties suitable for the garden, including 87 sweet peas.

At left: *Lathyrus odoratus*, sweet pea, found in many an old catalog, is still a favorite today. Above: The cypress vine, *Ipomoea quamoclit*, has feathery foliage and starlike flowers.

Eighty-nine years later, seeds of fewer than 200 annual flowers are offered by the same company, and the emphasis has changed from species to hybrid series.

The simple flower mignonette (*Reseda odorata*) was deemed worthy of eleven separate listings in Burpee's 1903 issue; 'Machet' (available today), 'New Golden Machet,' 'Improved Golden Queen', 'Allan's Defiance', 'Erfurt', 'Quaker City', 'Giant Flowered Red', 'Parson's White Tree', 'Giant Pyramidal', 'Improved Sweet' and 'Giant White Spiral'. To that list Park's 1904 *Floral Guide* added two more, 'Goliath' and 'Victoria'. One satisfied customer was prompted to write, "Mr. Park, Oh, the delightful fragrance and the modest beauty that lay dormant in a packet of your large-flowered Sweet Mignonette seeds!"

In tantalizing prose, period catalogs sing the praises of one annual flower after another: the moonflower's "rich Jessamine-like odor" (*Ipomoea alba*), the cypress vine's "elegant feathery foliage" and "scarlet flowers which stand out like constellations of stars" (*I. quamoclit*). No wonder we're unable to resist their admonition, "Let everyone possess themselves of it."

Unfortunately, most antique annuals have disappeared from commerce. A few names are familiar. 'Queen of the Market' China aster (*Callistephus chinensis*) and 'Empress of India' nasturtium (*Tropaeolum*), listed in Burpee's 1903 catalog as well as earlier editions, are still available. So are 'Crimson Giant' mignonette, listed in Buist's 1889 catalog, and the red and silver-white striped 'America' sweet pea (*Lathyrus odoratus*), listed in Prior's 1904 catalog. All appear in current listings of European seed houses.

Others, such as the striped globe amaranth (*Gomphrena globosa*), the bush dolichos, a non-twining hyacinth bean featured in Burpee's 1904 catalog (*Dolichos lablab*), the white-flowered cypress vine,

At left: Some antique varieties of *Gomphrena globosa*, globe amaranth, have disappeared from commerce. Above: *Callistephus chinensis*, China aster, is still available.

available as recently as 1989, and a marvel of Peru (*Mirabalis jalapa*) with "light green marbled leaves" are elusive and perhaps lost.

It's not only the venerable old-timers that fashion is passing by. The powder blue 'Blue Star' morning glory (*Ipomoea tricolor*) developed by Denholm Seeds in 1949 today is offered by only two or three seed merchants. 'Flying Saucers' morning glory, also a relative newcomer, can no longer be found. Antique as well as newer varieties continue to drop out of seed production and, therefore, seed catalogs at an alarming rate.

Once an antique annual is rediscovered, period catalogs provide the means to authenticate it. Trialing (growing the variety and comparing it with as many written descriptions and illustrations as possible) is also necessary. If all goes well, these varieties end up in my seed stocks and catalog and/or those of other heirloom seed merchants around the world, ready to flourish once again.

Searching for antique annuals is not the exclusive province of heirloom seed merchants, however. Heirloom seed exchanges, horticultural organizations' seed sales and agricultural market bulletins are additional sources which enable everyone to be a force for preservation. Seed merchants and gardeners can join forces to preserve our floral heritage. We can protect antique annuals from the vagaries of large commercial seed houses by enlisting experienced gardeners around the country to become contract growers of these endangered varieties, supplying small seed merchants who, in turn, supply the growing numbers of gardeners enamored of these precious plants.

For a complete list of flower seed exchanges, contact the American Horticultural Society's Gardener's Information Service, 1-800-777-7931, and ask for their bulletin "Heirloom Seed Resources."

ANNUALS FOR COOL CLIMATES

BY DAVID TARRANT

Nigella damascena

Brightly colored annuals are always associated with those hot days of high summer. In the southwest corner of British Columbia where I live, we rarely get the dog days of sum-

DAVID TARRANT *is the co-host of Canadian Broadcasting Corporation's popular* The Canadian Gardener, *the author of* A Year in Your Garden *(Whitecap, 1989),* Highrise Horticulture *(1989) and* David Tarrant's Pacific Gardening Guide *(1990). He writes for* The Vancouver Sun *and serves as education coordinator at the University of British Columbia Botanical Garden in Vancouver.*

mer so common in other areas of North America. And, contrary to popular opinion, it doesn't always rain here. We do get our fair share of moisture — something like 60 inches per year in Vancouver — but most of it falls during the fall and winter months, leaving July, August and September a good growing season for annuals.

We're not the only ones without sultry summers. Gardeners at high elevations and in northern latitudes also need annuals that perform in cool weather.

We have a good climate for many of the so-called hardy or half-hardy annuals — such plants as California poppies, Shirley

Left: *Papaver rhoeas,* the Shirley poppy.

Nigella damascena, love-in-a-mist, is usually blue. This one, called 'Cranberry', has dark pink flowers.

poppies, snapdragons and calendulas — which can easily be seeded directly in the garden. In fact, snapdragons and calendulas often self-seed.

Those familiar with reseeding annuals know the type — the ones that come up where they like. This gives them the reputation of being weedy, but my English roots tell me that they are the plants that produce the true cottage garden effect. You can always pull out the ones that "volunteer" in the wrong places.

If these plants are to be sown in a mixed border, prepare the ground at the end of the previous summer by adding a little well-rotted compost and turning it in. Trust me, if you wait until spring to enrich the soil the results will be poor. Don't overprepare; soil can be too well cultivated for most of the directly sown annuals. The time to direct sow is early in the season when the days are warm enough for the annual weeds to start germinating and the nights are still cool. In the Pacific Northwest this is late April.

Pot marigold (*Calendula officinalis*) forms a nice bushy plant two feet in height, with rich green foliage. The rayed flowers, up to four inches across, range from pale yellow to brilliant orange. The petals are edible and do much to brighten up a salad. The plants thrive in poor soil and full sun. There have been many new cultivars in recent years. The 'Bon Bon' mix offers flowers ranging from bright yellow and orange to delicate apricot and soft yellow.

Centaurea cyanus, commonly called bachelor buttons, is a slender annual reaching about two feet with narrow

Felicia amelloides, blue marguerite, which comes from South Africa, grows one to two feet high.

leaves and the most gorgeous blue flowers, although the inch-wide blossoms are sometimes purple, white or pink. They are superb cut flowers. Bachelor buttons must be grown in full sun in well-drained soil. Sown among solid orange calendulas, the dark blue cultivar 'Jubilee Gem' is stunning.

Consolida ambigua is the old favorite known to many of us as larkspur or annual delphinium. Delicate, feathery foliage covers the lower third of the branches below a spike of bright blue, pink or white flowers. It's a great one for cutting and also a good candidate for drying as it keeps its color well.

Cosmos bipinnatus is a rangy annual good for planting among other tall flowers towards the back of a mixed border. The flowers are true daises in white and pink to dark magenta. They cut well, and when seed is set later in the season they are a great attraction for birds.

Native to California, baby blue eyes (*Nemophila menziesii*) prefers semi-shade. It grows up to a foot in height with pinnate leaves and sky-blue flowers. I have had good success with it in patio containers. Some of the best plantings I have seen were in Skagway, Alaska.

By now you will know that I am addicted to blue flowers. The flowers of *Nigella damascena* are predominantly blue. The foliage is fennellike, clothing the stem and surrounding the flowers like a mist, hence the common name love-in-a-mist. In recent years I have fallen for one with dark pink flowers called 'Cranberry', and there is a good white form as well.

Shirley poppy (*Papaver rhoeas*) is a

Tropaeolum peregrinum, canary creeper, is a smaller cousin of nasturtium with handsome leaves and showy yellow flowers.

must for cooler climates. Not only does it thrive here, but it does well on the Atlantic coast and in mountainous regions. Some of the best plantings I have seen were on the Gaspe in Quebec and in New Brunswick. They are typical poppies with nodding buds. The petals have a tissue-paper quality. The flowers are up to three inches across and range from white through pink to dark rose. In recent years there have been strains introduced, such as 'Fairy Wings', with delicate, muted colors.

The glaucous foliage of opium poppy (*Papaver somniferum*) forms a pretty rosette at the base of the plant, and leaves appear all the way up the three-foot stems. The flowers are large, sometimes double and a bit blowsy. I prefer the singles which can be delicate mauve, pure white and many shades of red.

Reseda odorata is commonly called mignonette but sadly is not commonly grown. It is not a showy annual but it is highly fragrant. The plant is short — no more than ten inches tall — and falls about a bit. The foliage is somewhat like small spinach and the flower spikes are greenish yellow and brown. It must be sown near patio doors or windows for sheer summer evening sensuous delight.

Nasturtium (*Tropaeolum majus)* is a terrific annual for cooler climes. There are now bushy forms but the typical habit is trailing. The leaves are attractive, like flat circular umbrellas, and the flowers are three inches across and spurred at the back. They come in a wide range of colors and are sweetly scented.

Canary creeper (*Tropaeolum pere-*

Nicotiana alata, flowering tobacco, is usually white and a bit rangy in growth habit. 'Nikki' is a newer, more compact form with pink to red flowers.

grinum) is a smaller cousin of the nasturtium. Its yellow flowers are only one inch across but many and showy, set off by handsome lobed leaves. It climbs over other plants well, and if used on a trellis it will provide quick summer privacy.

Tender Perennials

Many of the direct-sown annuals are not season-long performers. A variety of tender perennials can help prolong the summer display. For these annuals, which are started indoors or purchased and planted out for the summer, good soil preparation is a definite must. Add either well rotted manure or compost to the area in late fall or early spring.

Fibrous begonia (*Begonia semperflorens*) comes into its own during August, blooming until frost. It forms a bushy plant with shiny, waxlike leaves and masses of tiny flowers. There are many horticultural forms, some with dark red foliage and others with light green. These plants do best in a semishaded spot, although they grow well in full sun with adequate moisture. Fibrous begonias root well from cuttings and may even be wintered inside as houseplants.

Callistephus chinensis, better known as China aster, reminds me of my childhood as they were a popular plant in southern England. They are easy to grow, extremely showy and invaluable for cutting. The overall height is 18 inches to two feet. They are basically single-stemmed daisies three to four inches across, several per plant, in a range of colors. I prefer the single types.

Blue marguerite (*Felicia amelloides*) comes from South Africa and is anywhere from one to two feet in height, bushy, with

Nemesia strumosa, a showy annual at its best in early summer, is a good container plant.

rough, hairy leaves. The blue daisy flowers have bright yellow centers and measure half an inch across. There are white-flowered forms and one with striking variegated leaves is worth looking for. Propagate from cuttings and overwinter in a cool greenhouse.

Impatiens walleriana, sometimes called busy lizzie, is valuable because it comes into its best from August through September. Even in our cooler climate it requires shade. Most garden cultivars reach anywhere from six inches to two feet. The plants are bushy with succulent stems and small leaves. The flowers are one to two inches across in white, red, pink and deeper shades of rose. Some of the more recent introductions are in designer shades of purple and hot pink. They overwinter well from cuttings.

Rose mallow (*Lavatera trimestris*) is a wonderful annual mallow that attains three feet in height with angled leaves about two inches across and many large rose-pink flowers three inches across. It is a must for any mixed border. A gorgeous white form is called 'Mont Blanc'. I have seen superb beds of this plant in Alaska and Nova Scotia.

Nemesia strumosa is a very showy annual known widely by its botanical name. It is one of those early-summer showstoppers that is usually past its best by mid-August. It forms erect but bushy plants a foot to 18 inches in height. Masses of bright flowers, one inch across, cluster at the top of each stem above narrow leaves. *Nemesia* is a good annual for pots.

Flowering tobacco (*Nicotiana alata*) has large basal leaves like those of fox-

Nolana paradoxa is a spreading plant that does well at the front of the border or in pots.

glove and long rangy stems to three feet carrying the sweetly scented, trumpetlike blossoms. The flowers are two inches long and about one and a half inches across. A dandy cultivar for flower arranging, 'Nikki Lime' has chartreuse flowers. Recent introductions, such as the 'Nikki', 'Domino' and 'Starship' strains, are shorter and more manageable for smaller home gardens. They should be in every mixed flower border in cooler climates.

Nolana paradoxa is another one of my blue favorites. I was first introduced to it in a Nova Scotia garden, where I was impressed by its bright, dark blue flowers with a whitish to pale yellow throat. *Nolana* is a spreading plant up to 18 inches in height, and it grows well in containers and is invaluable for the front of a border.

Osteospermun amplectans is another South African native that thrives in this climate, but its showy daisies only open on sunny days. The plant reaches about 18 inches and tends to fall about, forming attractive loose clumps. The flowers are two inches across and range from creamy white through yellow to apricot, with shiny black centers. It is a spectacular annual and deserves to be grown more widely.

Tagetes filifolia is one of the many marigolds known to gardeners. This particular one is my favorite because it forms a small compact bush up to a foot in height with fine foliage and many tiny, half inch, bright orange or yellow flowers. It was the old standby edging marigold and is still as valuable as ever. One thing in particular in this marigold's favor for Northwest gardens is its tolerance of rain.

ANNUAL STYLE IN THE WARM-WEATHER GARDEN

BY TOM PEACE

Zea mays

The midsummer garden is a wonderful canvas on which to paint your passions and personality, just as clothes, cuisine and decor display individual style for others to enjoy. Not many gardeners see this sometimes difficult season as an opportunity to express themselves. Perhaps it is because too many see petunias, pansies and marigolds as the only options for summer color; and to make matters worse, these plants rarely survive the entire season, often passing out from the heat and spider mites.

Few gardeners realize just how flexible their "permanent" borders can become by adding annuals. Each summer is a new opportunity to imbue the garden with fresh colors, textures and themes. Bulbs and early-blooming perennials such as delphinium, poppy, iris and lupine, which have played out by June, can share space in the border with annuals for the summer. With an expanded palette of heat-tolerant annual flowers and foliage, the summer garden

TOM PEACE, *a landscape designer, writer and nurseryman, designs gardens in Arizona, Colorado and Texas.*

Left: A spectacular combination for the warm-weather garden: *Ricinus communis*, castor bean, *Gladiolus callianthus* and *Monarda*, beebalm.

Cleome hassleriana, spider flower, which grows six to ten feet high, is a good candidate for the back of the border.

becomes an ideal setting in which to express personal style — even in areas with stiflingly hot summers.

Hot weather, for plants, is defined more by night than by day temperatures, and it is important to wait until the weather warms sufficiently before planting out heat-loving flowers. Follow the rule of thumb for peppers in the vegetable garden: wait for 60-degree night temperatures before setting them out. Over-eager spring planting of some heat lovers will stunt the plants and slow their performance for the rest of the season. Impatiens planted after the last frost (but while the weather is still cool) will be only half the size of those planted three weeks later (with warmer night temperatures) when the two are compared in August. So relax and enjoy the late-spring blooms without feeling the need to plant for summer until the weather is warm. Then let your imagination run wild and transform your garden into a colorful summer paradise.

Hot-weather annuals include three different plant types: tender perennials (such as *Verbena bonariensis* or *Salvia farinacea*) which are hardy from zone seven south, tropicals (the likes of *Coleus* and *Caladium*) and true annuals (*Portulaca, Perilla* or *Ageratum,* for example). There will be some overlap. Some of the tropical or tender perennials may be shrubs or even trees in their native habitats, but in our gardens for the summer they stay much smaller.

While annuals by definition are expendable components of the mixed border, you may want to make an effort to hold over a few favorite tropicals or tender perennials (if they won't survive under a heavy mulch). Once I got hold of my princess flower (*Tibouchina urvilleana*), I always found a spot inside the house for it to spend the winter, and it also became the mother of many new plants from cuttings. *Hymenocallis*, caladiums, cannas, summer callas and tuberous begonias all can be stored easily for the winter, so a one-time expenditure produces an excellent yield of summer pleasure over the years.

Easy annuals can be regenerated yearly from seed, so do be sure to collect some seed for yourself and your friends. The adventurous gardener may have to hunt around a bit for the less familiar catalogs featuring unusual annuals, but the extra effort is worth it.

After a long, cold winter with scanty horticultural relief, I tend to overcompensate in the summer months. Sometimes it is all I can do to keep from planting the parlor palm out where the poppies and delphiniums have finished their spring show. I do, however, always manage to find a place for castor beans (*Ricinus communis*), cannas and corn (that's right, *Zea mays* — more on this in a minute).

Of these three, cannas require the least room in the border and fit right in where the June bloomers have retreated. The canna's unfortunate history of misuse has led many gardeners to view this flower with disdain, but I find its foliage and form to be a refreshing ingredient in the border, especially when combined with some of the larger ornamental grasses like *Miscanthus* or *Pennisetum*. Statuesque red-leaved castor beans provide the backbone for such a combination; in roomier gardens, the six to ten foot plants also look stunning amidst woodland tobacco (*Nicotiana sylvestris*) with its large chartreuse leaves, and pink or white spider flower

Large ornamental grasses such as *Miscanthus sinensis* 'Variegatus', left, and *Pennisetum setaceum*, right, also make statuesque backdrops for the border.

Castor bean is a dramatic accent against a terra cotta-colored wall.
Give this plant plenty of room.

(*Cleome hassleriana*). Add a few dozen fragrant, white-flowered Abyssinian gladiolus (*Gladiolus callianthus*) and 'Italian White' sunflowers for a cool-looking, dramatic planting.

Corn was the first grass I fell in love with, long before big ornamental grasses were in vogue. I am still impressed by its ability to grow so tall so quickly, but successful use in the border depends on planting tight clumps rather than rows as in ear production. If you like autumn-colored foliage, try the Indian corn which turns rich burgundy-red as it ripens, contrasting with the late blue blooms of *Salvia guaranitica* or *S.* 'Indigo Spires' and golden *Rudbeckia triloba* in the foreground. Otherwise, choose the tallest variety of corn that you can find, such as 'Silver Queen', which rises to eight or nine feet in just a few hot months and is reminiscent of timber bamboo.

Moving out of the land of the giants to midsized plants, I recommend tall verbena (*V. bonariensis*). This plant is a nonstop performer but needs to be planted in small groups, at least, for the airy, three- to five-foot stems to carry their weight in the garden. Tall verbena's purple heads contrast perfectly with yellow, orange or red cannas and by Hawaiian hibiscus (*Hibiscus rosa-sinensis*).

Dahlias finally fit in with the rest of the summer garden, no longer needing to be segregated in another bed due to the outlandish scale of their frisbee-sized flowers. The relatively new class of border dahlias offers a wide range of bloom colors. The pastel varieties of these sun worshipers from Mexico look at home in cottage gardens with daylilies and baby's breath, and their brighter counterparts can add pizzazz to sassier combinations.

Salvias are the wave of the future for hot-weather gardens. Although most salvias are perennial in Zone 7 and south, some are easily used as annuals for summer color farther north. The average gardener knows only scarlet *S. splendens* and blue *S. farinacea*. The sub-shrub cherry sage (*S. greggii*) is now available in creamy white, coral, pink and purple in addition to its original red-flowered form. Cherry sage tolerates heat and drought. I plant it in drier soils with yellow creeping zinnia (*Sanvitalia procumbens*) and moss rose (*Portulaca* hybrids); it harmonizes well with pale yellow *Coreopsis* 'Moonbeam' and blue *Ageratum* 'Cut Wonder' in soils with more moisture. Another Zone 8 perennial used as an annual, scarlet sage (*S. coccinea*) produces orange-red flowers on terminal, three to four foot spikes from midsummer until frost. It tolerates some shade, so don't be afraid to try it under trees with woodland tobacco and *Rudbeckia triloba*, punctuated by red-leaved caladiums for a stunning effect.

Heat-loving annual additions to the border aren't all hot colored, so there is hope for those who abhor reds and oranges. Both the blue plumbago (*Plumbago auriculata*) and Mexican heather (*Cuphea hyssopifolia*) are Zone 8 perennials that can be used as annuals in the north with wonderful results. Few flowers compare with plumbago's sky blue, phloxlike clusters on the end of arching stems, and the plant blooms easily in the sun at an early age. Mexican heather already will be showing its small violet flowers by the time it's available at local garden centers, and will continue to bloom all summer until the first hard frost. With pink fountain grass (*Pennisetum alopecuroides*) or the white form of Madagascar periwinkle (*Catharanthus roseus*) these plants comprise a well-balanced triad that thrives on heat — even in a ferocious Texan summer — while looking cool and refreshing. Like the periwinkle, globe amaranth (*Gomphrena globosa*) from India is undaunted by oppressive heat and humidity and comes in a cool spectrum of pastel pink, white, peach and violet clover-flowered cultivars. These plants mix prettily with lavender weeping lantana (*Lantana montevidensis*) which shares globe amaranth's amazing ability to withstand the heat. Silvery foliage from dusty miller (*Senecio cineraria*) and bright pink geraniums (pelargoniums are overused but do perform well in the heat) complete this cool-toned ensemble for continuous bloom even when the weather bakes.

Many of the more unusual plants tend toward the fiery hues. One particularly dramatic combination uses Mexican sunflower (*Tithonia rotundifolia*), a large, branching annual with furry leaves and brilliant orange daisylike flowers, flanked by standing cypress (*Ipomopsis rubra*) with feathery foliage on tall vertical stems crowned by clusters of scarlet trumpets, and *Nicotiana langsdorfii* with its nodding green bells thrown in for a bit of contrast.

Another orange bloomer from south of the border is the Mexican fire bush (*Hamelia patens*), a tropical tree used as a perennial in the South and as an annual in colder climates. Fire bush demands hot weather and will sulk in temperatures below 85 degrees, but also requires ample moisture for good growth. A daring soul could try fire bush in a hot spot with purple Mexican bush sage (*Salvia leucantha*), which blooms in late summer, purple border dahlias and a carpet of *Gazania rigens*. Or, if your favorite color is orange, plant Mexican sunflower and fire bush and *Canna* 'Wyoming' with cigar plant (*Cuphea ignea*) in the foreground.

Whether you favor cool, pastel colors or warm, fiery tones, make the most of your border with annuals for nonstop summer bloom.

FAVORITE ANNUAL CUT FLOWERS

BY RITA BUCHANAN

Cosmos bipinnatus

Like many people, I rarely have enough time to just sit outdoors and enjoy my garden. I do the chores — water and weed, plant and pull — then hurry off to work or to a meeting, to cook or to shop. Since I can't linger in the garden, I've learned to bring the garden indoors by growing loads of flowers for cutting. The reward is surprisingly rich. Appreciating the flowers in a vase on my desk is a focused and intimate experience that lasts for hours as I sit there at work. I never sit still for so long outdoors. Who does nowadays?

Annuals provide a wonderful assortment of cut flowers, and they're easy and inexpensive to grow. You can start with transplants from local garden centers, but arranging is more fun when you've got a wide selection of flowers. For more variety, grow your own plants from seed. I study

RITA BUCHANAN *grows annuals and herbs in her Connecticut garden, writes for several magazines and edits gardening books for Houghton Mifflin. She was guest editor of BBG's handbook* Dyes from Nature, *published in 1990.*

Left: To last as a cut flower, cosmos, *Cosmos bipinnatus*, must be placed in warm water and stored in a cool room overnight.

the catalogs and order everything that looks interesting, then start just a dozen or so plants of each variety or color. (To save the extra seeds for future seasons, I seal the packets with some silica gel desiccant in moisture-tight containers and store them in a cool, dark place.) I start snapdragons, salvias and other small-seeded and slow-growing annuals indoors under fluorescent lights but direct-sow zinnias, cosmos, calendulas and other fast growers.

The plants described in this article are some of my favorites. In addition to form and color, I look for long stems and a vase life of at least several days in plain water; adding a floral preservative to the water can double the average vase life.

These annuals all grow best in well-tilled, fertile soil with steady moisture and full sun. On average, the plants need a square foot of garden space each. You can combine annuals with other plants in mixed borders and beds, or make a separate cutting garden. A four by 25 foot bed will hold about a hundred plants and provide armloads of bouquets. For easy care and access, I plant flowers for cutting in beds no wider than four feet.

Spring Posies

Pansies, pinks and globe candytuft are some of the first annuals to bloom in spring. They're all small plants and the flowers are rather short-stemmed, but they make charming, long-lived nosegays.

Pansies (*Viola* x *wittrockiana*) are very cold-hardy but don't take heat well. Gardeners in mild climates can plant pansies in the fall for winter and spring bloom. In colder regions, plant pansies at daffodil time. Cultivars differ in flower color, and the flowers may be solid or have contrasting spots. Dark red and purple pansies are often fragrant. Pansy flower size and stem length are variable. As young plants, 'Swiss Giants' or other large-flowered cultivars

Pansies look lovely floating in a shallow dish.

start bearing flowers up to four inches wide, on stems as short as four inches. These look lovely floating in a shallow dish. Later, the very same plants will make one-inch flowers on eight-inch stems.

The annual China pinks (*Dianthus chinensis*) begin blooming as early as ten weeks from sowing and continue all summer. They bear clusters of dime-sized flowers in bright pinks, reds and white; some have striped, fringed or picoteed petals. The 'Telstar' hybrids grow about ten inches tall; they branch at the base, so you can cut entire stems.

Globe candytufts (*Iberis umbellata*) also bloom quickly from seed. The plants form a low mound of a dozen or more stems, each topped with a generous cluster of small white, pink or rosy flowers. The flat

Dianthus chinensis, China pinks, bloom in clusters of dime-sized flowers in shades of pink, red and white. Some are striped, fringed or picoteed.

papery fruits (green at first, ripening to a warm gold) develop so quickly that a single stem usually carries all stages from bud to pod. The stems are short, never reaching 12 inches, but both flowers and pods are easy to appreciate.

Fragrant Flowers

Many annuals are mildly scented. The ones mentioned below are especially fragrant (although floral fragrances can be elusive; intensity often varies with temperature and time of day). Within a plant species, different cultivars and color selections may be more or less fragrant. Keep trying until you find a kind you like.

Stocks, sweet williams and carnations all have a warm, spicy fragrance. Among stocks (*Matthiola incana*), I've had better luck with the ten-week types than with the taller, slower Brompton selections. My ten-week stocks usually bloom in 12 to 16 weeks from seed, with dense upright spikes of tender-petalled flowers in shades of pink, rose, purple and white. Cool temperatures and short days promote the best flowering. In mild climates, the seedlings will overwinter outdoors. Here in Connecticut, I start stocks indoors in late winter and set them out in early spring.

The related night-scented stock (*M. bicornis*) isn't much to look at, with its weak gray stems and sparse lavender flowers that close during the day, but its fragrance is intensely sweet. Tuck one or two stems in an arrangement to fill a room with aroma. Night-scented stocks have an internal clock: even after cutting, they open up

47

and release their fragrance only at night and close again in the morning.

Old-fashioned sweet Williams (*Dianthus barbatus*) are biennials or short-lived perennials. I sow the seeds in August for bloom the following May and June, and usually start new plants each year. The richly scented flowers are clustered in heads three to five inches wide atop 20-inch stems, and easily last two weeks in water. Individual plants yield a dozen or more stems. There are also annual sweet Williams. They've tended to be dwarf plants with weak stems and scentless flowers, but 'New Era' is a new annual sweet William from Thompson and Morgan, who claim it grows 24 to 30 inches tall with fragrant flowers in May from a February sowing.

Carnations (*Dianthus caryophyllus*) can be tricky. The stems are floppy, the plants are subject to fungal diseases and many cultivars are scentless. But I've been quite pleased with the carnation 'Fragrance', a mix of compact, upright plants with spicy, two-inch flowers in shades of pink or white. From an indoor sowing in March, they bloom from July to hard frost. In water, the flowers last seven to ten days.

Sweet peas (*Lathyrus odoratus*) have penetratingly sweet fragrance. They do best in rich soil, prefer cool weather and generally need a trellis or support. Dig deep and add plenty of compost, then direct-sow the seeds about two inches apart in very early spring. With an early start, the vines grow quickly up to six feet tall and bloom before the heat of summer. (Among sweet peas, "heat tolerant" means the plants tolerate days in the 80's if the nights are cool.) Most cultivars produce about six flowers per bunch in shades of white, pink and lavender. The old-fashioned kinds with smaller flowers are more fragrant than the newer large-flowered varieties.

Sweet sultan (*Centaurea moschata*) does

RITA BUCHANAN

Sweet William, foreground, easily lasts two weeks in water.

fine in ordinary or even poor soil and tolerates heat and dryness. I sow seeds outdoors after the last frost and thin to six-inch spacing. The plants grow about two feet tall and bear lavender, white or yellow flowers resembling two-inch powderpuffs. Cut the flowers just as they open to enjoy their fresh sweet fragrance for several days indoors.

Sweet scabious or pincushion flowers (*Scabiosa atropurpurea*) are clustered in two-inch heads on long, wiry stems. Like sweet sultan, the plants grow about two feet tall. The flowers are more profuse, are borne over a longer season and last longer in water, but they don't smell quite as sweet. Sweet scabious come in shades of pink, lavender, blue and white.

It's easy to overlook the tiny reddish flowers of mignonette (*Reseda odorata*),

The carnation *Dianthus caryophyllus* 'Fragrance' has spicy, two-inch flowers in shades of pink or white. As cut flowers, they last seven to ten days.

but you can't miss their sweet scent. I've read that French homemakers used to keep a single stem in water to perfume a room through the winter months. Those rooms were probably chilly; at room temperature in my house, cut mignonettes only last a week or two. Mignonettes are leafy plants that wilt or die back in hot, dry weather. They bloom quickly from seed, so I sow them in early spring and again in midsummer for fall fragrance.

Fillers

By fillers, I mean delicate blossoms useful for filling the spaces between larger, showier flowers. One airy filler is bishop's flower (*Ammi majus*), a bushy annual with fernlike leaves and flat-topped clusters of tiny white flowers that look just like the biennial wild carrot or Queen Anne's lace. Start bishop's flower seeds indoors or sow directly in the garden; do both to extend the period of bloom.

Annual baby's breath (*Gypsophila elegans*) has larger flowers — up to one-half inch wide — than the perennial kind. The stems are delicate and branch repeatedly, making the flowers appear to float in space. 'Covent Garden' has chalky white flowers. 'Rosea' is a pink form. Neither dries well, and the plants tend to bloom themselves out quickly, so you'll need to resow every few weeks for flowers throughout the season.

Annual statice (*Limonium sinuatum*), well known as an everlasting, is also a fine fresh cut flower. I start the seed early indoors and set them out when the soil

49

gets warm. The leaf rosettes stay remarkably flat for several weeks and often grow wider than dinnerplates before flowering starts. Then each plant produces several flower stalks two to three feet tall. Color ranges widely, from white and yellow to rosy pink, lavender and blue.

Spikes

These annuals bear flowers in slender upright spikes. All start blooming at the bottom and proceed to the top, with individual flowers opening over a period of up to two weeks.

Children love to snap the hinged blossoms of old-fashioned single snapdragons (*Antirrhinum majus*). The newer forms with frilly double flowers are more showy but less playful. Many snapdragons, especially the dark red ones, smell like Kool-Aid. All are excellent cut flowers. The seeds and seedlings are small, so I start them in February and set them out a few weeks before the last frost date. (Transplants can take a bit of frost; mature plants overwinter in mild climates.) Pinching the seedlings promotes branching at the base and multiple flower stalks. Hilling a mound of soil around the base of the plants as they grow keeps the stalks from tipping over. The plants may rest after first blooming in early summer — cut off the old flower-stalks and they'll bloom again into the fall.

Larkspurs are often described as annual delphiniums, with dense spikes of flat, double, inch-wide flowers in bright blues, pinks and white. Cultivars of the three common species (*Consolida ambigua, C. orientalis* and *C. regalis*) differ in height, branching, spike density and time of first bloom. All do best when direct-sown in fall or early spring. They resent transplanting, even if you're careful not to disturb the roots. Larkspurs are good both as fresh cut flowers and as everlastings; indeed, they often dry in the vase with no special care. The petals

Snapdragons come in many forms and make excellent cut flowers.

hold their color well but shatter easily.

Two popular cultivars of mealy-cup sage (*Salvia farinacea*) form finger-sized spikes of tiny flowers atop strong, slender stems. 'Victoria' has blue flowers; 'White Bedder' is white. Start these in a warm spot indoors and transplant the seedlings after danger of frost. Both grow up to three feet tall and flower steadily for months. Native Texas perennials, they are usually grown as annuals in gardens. Like larkspurs, these salvia flowers last well indoors.

Tricolor sage (*Salvia viridis*, formerly *S. horminum*) is an annual that can be direct-sown in warm soil. It's a straggly plant with scratchy stems, and the actual flowers are insignificant. What matters are the clusters of bright pink, blue, lavender or cream bracts that sail like flags atop two-foot

Leucanthemum x *superbum* 'Starburst', a short-lived perennial best used as an annual, has cheery white flowers on long, straight stems.

stalks. These hold their color well, and are lovely fresh or dried.

Bells-of-Ireland (*Moluccella laevis*) also has a prickly texture and insignificant flowers, but it makes wonderful thick, dense spikes. Each green bell is the expanded calyx of an otherwise tiny flower. Bells-of-Ireland seeds require a few weeks of cool temperatures and light to germinate, and the seedlings don't transplant well. Sow them outdoors in early spring, cover with a very thin layer of vermiculite, and keep them moist. Once started, the plants grow quickly with no special care and grow two to three feet tall.

Daisies and other Composites

Everyone likes daisies and similar flowers, called composites. Most are very easy to grow, flower abundantly and offer cheery round flower clusters on long, straight stems.

For classic daisies with yellow disks and white rays, try *Leucanthemum* x *superbum* 'Snow Lady' and 'Starburst'. Both plants are short-lived perennials liable to rot in wet winters, so I grow them as annuals. They flower in mid-summer from a March sowing indoors. 'Snow Lady' has daisies two to three inches wide and grows one foot tall. 'Starburst' has daisies five to six inches wide and grows up to 30 inches tall. The most common form of the herb feverfew (*Chrysanthemum parthenium*) has branching stems topped with dozens of miniature daisies and blooms off and on from summer through late fall. Other plants also called feverfew (*Matricaria inodora*) have spherical white or yellow flowerheads. All last very well as cut flowers.

Yarrow (*Achillea millefolium*) is another perennial that blooms in its first year. The 'Summer Pastels' series includes shades of cream, pink, yellow, coral and lilac. From a basal rosette of fernlike foliage, stems two feet tall carry flat clusters of tiny daisylike blossoms. Sow the tiny seeds indoors in February and you'll have plants that bloom from July through late fall. Cut when about half the blossoms on a head have opened for fresh or everlasting bouquets.

'Gloriosa daisies' (garden tetraploids developed from the annual black-eyed Susan, *Rudbeckia hirta*) grow two to three feet tall with flower heads up to six inches wide. Some are yellow with brown eyes, others are rusty red, gold, mahogany or bicolored. Start the seed indoors or sow directly in warm soil. Space 18 inches apart, as the plants get rather large and the foliage is prone to mildew if plants are crowded. Cut or deadhead regularly to prolong blooming from summer to fall.

Zinnias, cosmos, calendulas, china asters and dahlias are all easy-to-grow favorites. All transplant easily from seedlings started indoors, or grow quickly if direct-seeded after frost. In every case, to grow flowers for cutting, shun those super-dwarf varieties with flowers wider than the stems are long. Look for standard types that grow at least two feet tall.

Among zinnias, I like the 'Ruffles' series, a cut-and-come-again type of *Zinnia elegans* with three-inch, double flowers in scarlet, pink, yellow and white. 'Persian Carpet' and 'Old Mexico' (both cultivars of *Z. haageana*) have smaller, multicolored flowers. Be sure to strip all the leaves off zinnia stems, as they turn to smelly mush if submerged in a vase.

Cosmos bipinnatus 'Sensation' comes in dark and pale pinks and white, with flowers three to four inches wide on plants three to four feet tall. *Cosmos* 'Sonata' has similar

Larkspur is a good fresh-cut flower or can be dried as an everlasting.

flowers on smaller plants. Although I've often read that cosmos make wonderful cut flowers, mine always seemed to wilt quickly. Then I learned that they must be conditioned — placed in a deep bucket of warm water and stored in a cool room overnight. Given that treatment, they last a good week in arrangements.

Growing dahlias (*Dahlia* hybrids) from seed is less predictable but more economical than buying tubers. The plants grow mounds of foliage in the heat of summer, then bloom profusely during the shorter days and cooler temperatures of late August through fall. Choose tall varieties with cactus, pompon or daisy-type flowers. Seed packets generally include a mix of yellow, pink and red. Plunge cut dahlias up to their necks in hot tap water for 20 to 30

Zinnia elegans 'Ruffles' can be cut time and again and will continue to send up its three-inch, double flowers.

minutes, until the stem turns dark gray-green, to increase their vase life by several days.

China asters (*Callistephus chinensis*) can be easy or impossible to grow, depending on whether or not your garden soil is contaminated with fungal diseases. (Some cultivars are wilt-resistant, but most asters are quite vulnerable to disease.) Given disease-free soil, direct-sown asters bloom from late July to frost in shades of white, pink, lavender and purple. There are daisylike single asters with yellow disks, and double forms that resemble fluffy pompons. All make excellent cut flowers.

Last of the season, and perhaps the best cut flowers of all, are garden chrysanthemums. The plants aren't reliably hardy here where winters are cold and wet, so I grow three cultivars as annuals. *Chrysanthemum koreanum* 'Fanfare' starts blooming in late summer and continues into fall, with clusters of double flowers two to three inches wide atop long branched stems. *C. indicum* 'Super Jet' grows three feet tall, with stems branching near the top to bear dozens of three-inch, double flowers in solid shades of cream, yellow, gold, pink, rust and red. *C. i.* 'Petit Point' has similar stems, but the two-inch blossoms are single, like daisies, with yellow disks and colored rays. Both bloom late, when the fall foliage is at its peak. Even in Connecticut, mums provide cut flowers until Halloween, and sometime bouquets last indoors until Thanksgiving. At that point it's only a short wait until the seed catalogs arrive with promise of next year's season.

ANNUALS WITH FINE FOLIAGE

BY ANGELA OVERY

E u p h o r b i a   m a r g i n a t a

The phrase "foliage annuals" sounds like a contradiction in terms. Most people think of annuals as the bright stars of the garden, the bold-colored flowers that liven up the solid foundation of trees, shrubs and perennials.

ANGELA OVERY, *an illustrator and writer, is the author of* The Foliage Garden *(Harmony, 1993) and contributes to many gardening magazines. She is co-director of the Denver Botanic Garden's School of Botanical Illustration. She lives and gardens in Sedalia, Colorado.*

However, foliage annuals are indispensable in today's garden. They serve a number of purposes, from disguising unsightly views to creating a lush tropical paradise on a suburban patio.

The term "annual" here has been broadly used to include genuine annuals (which grow from seed, flower and die in one season), perennials that can be used as annuals in climates in which they are not reliably hardy and tuberous plants that can be wintered over indoors.

Foliage annuals can be used to create temporary screens in a great hurry, as well

Left: The spectacular dark red foliage of castor bean sets off deep pink perennial phlox in this mixed border.

as to embellish arbors and trellises. Scarlet runner bean (*Phaseolus coccineus*) is a good choice; its plentiful foliage offers leafy shade, while its red flowers and delicious pods are a bonus. Hyacinth bean (*Dolichos lablab*), which has bronze-purple blushed leaves, pretty pink flowers and an edible bean, will fulfill the same function.

Two tall annuals grow extremely quickly and thus can be used as dramatic backdrops to a border, as bold accents or to screen eyesores. The first is *Ricinus communis*, the castor bean plant from tropical Africa. Its large seeds are sometimes said to resemble ticks, but everything else about this plant, though oversized, is wel-

come. The castor bean plant reaches the size of a small tree or shrub when grown as an annual, with large, palmately compound leaves. It grows with Jack-and-the-beanstalk-like speed — as high as twenty feet in humid climates, about half as high in arid ones. There are green and handsome bronze varieties, such as 'Zanzibarensis'. Another exotic-looking African native is *Hibiscus acetosella* 'Red Shield', which rapidly grows to about five feet high and has dark maroon leaves.

Nothing makes a dense, annual hedge like the fat, roundish burning bush (*Kochia scoparia* var. *trichophylla*). Ideal for planting while waiting for a more stately box or yew hedge to grow, the bright green, four- to five-foot high burning bush turns purple and finally a "hell fire and brimstone" red in fall. Since you're growing it for only one season, you may as well have fun with it.

You may also be amused by the three annuals sometimes called beefsteak plant, thanks to their raw beef color laced with meatlike veins. The most bizarre is *Acalypha wilkesiana* of the Euphorbia family. It is a tropical plant from the Malay Archipelago, named after Charles Wilkes, an American explorer of the Pacific. The tender plant can be grown in a greenhouse or in flower beds or containers for an unusual effect. The toothed edges of some variegated types have handsome pale margins, and other varieties have interesting scrumpled and puckered leaves — like pieces of brilliantly colored fabric cut with pinking shears and bunched together.

Perilla frutescens is a shrubby annual herb from the Orient, sometimes nicknamed beefsteak, but prettier than the connotation and thus often called Chinese basil. Use perilla to introduce small blocks of a metallic, coppery purple to a bed or pot. It looks lovely with pale blue or pink flowers, and quite sophisticated with gray foliage.

Red-veined calladium and chartreuse coleus are standouts in this container garden.

The third beefsteak plant is *Iresine herbstii*, a tender perennial also called blood leaf. An old-fashioned house plant with dark red and pink leaves, when moved outdoors it can be a striking addition to the shady summer garden.

Dusty miller (*Senecio cineraria*) is another plant that has been around a long time, and is probably the first plant which comes to mind when foliage annuals are discussed. Its popularity is well deserved. The silvery foliaged charmer is a foil for brightly colored flowering annuals and an obvious choice for mixed plantings in pots. Mine have overwintered in the kitchen window nestled among pink-flowering pelargoniums, and it survives outdoors in some regions. A newer plant, which is also called dusty miller on occasion, is *Artemisia stelleriana*, one of the tender perennial artemisias often grown as annuals. It too has soft, gray foliage.

The delicate tones of silvery gray and turquoise blue of the dusty millers can help calm down the bright tropical foliage of *Amaranthus tricolor*, with aptly named cultivars such as 'Joseph's Coat' and 'Molten Fire'. These many-colored herbs can add drama to any garden situation. Purple heart (*Setcreasea pallida*) is another tropical immigrant with silvery purple leaves. Red orache (*Atriplex hortensis*) is a fast-growing, four- to six-foot tall, red-leaved annual that can be sown directly in the border. The strong-colored foliage can be helpful in beds that do not have sufficient shape or structure.

Foliage annuals need not be brightly colored. Two subtler-toned plants I consider well worth growing are feverfew (*Chrysanthemum parthenium* 'Aureum'), for its mounds of lime green foliage and white button blossoms, and American native snow-on-the-mountain (*Euphorbia marginata*), a vigorous annual grown easily from seed with crisp striped green and white bracts and leaves.

Many of the annual vegetables are finding their way into borders and patio pots, where their foliage, when it is not eaten, adds interesting texture and style. Three of the best are fennel (*Foeniculum vulgare*), which produces airy clouds of green or purple foliage, cabbage (*Brassica oleracea*) and beautiful lettuces, such as *Lactuca sativa* 'Rosy', which has a green iceberg-lettucelike center and delicately frilled mauve outer leaves.

Two thistles are often admired for their wonderful spiky foliage. *Silybum marianum*, milk thistle, displays marbleized green leaves and is about three to four feet

Coleus and asparagus add accent, form and texture to this container planting.

In this intriguing foliage combination, *Ptilostemon afer*, a spiny herb, is planted with *Perilla frutescens* 'Purpurea'.

high, while *Onopordum acanthium*, Scottish thistle, a biennial, is an architectural colossus with huge, hairy, silvery leaves. A pair of grasses should be added to any list of fine foliage annuals for the sunny border: *Pennisetum villosum*, feather top, and the larger *Pennisetum setaceum*, fountain grass, add grace and height to summer plantings.

The many brightly colored *Coleus* x *hybridus* grown in place of blooming annuals are something of a cliche in a shady garden. Planted in blocks of color, or in clever combinations, however, they can be lively. 'Red Velvet', for instance, looks downright theatrical planted with Japanese painted fern and red-leaved fibrous begonias, and there is a good yellow coleus called 'Pineapple Wizard', which gleams beside pale buttery yellow annuals. There

is even a black coleus, which has a good deal of *savoir-faire* planted beside chartreuse feverfew.

If your garden tends toward the fashionable perennials, the place to experiment with some of the intriguing foliage annuals is in pots and baskets, which can be moved about and brought indoors before the first frost. Some of my favorites are the dwarf cannas (*Canna* x *generalis*) which are really tender perennials and need rich soil and lots of water and fertilizer. Their bright green or burgundy-red leaves are wrapped and folded in neat spikes, like table napkins in a restaurant. They look their best amid frothy annuals which spill out of the pots, like lobelia (*Lobelia erinus*) or sweet alyssum (*Lobularia maritima*). Tall cannas are also excellent at the back of a tropical looking border.

A plethora of annuals with interesting foliage, from multicolored croton to rex begonia to ornamental sweet potato, tumble out of a windowbox.

Elephant ear (*Colocasia esculenta*) has emerald-green, elephantine leaves luxuriant enough to turn a cement or stone patio into a bit of Hawaii, although it needs afternoon shade in most climates and constant moisture. Combine it with pots of *Caladium* x *hortulanum*, tropical tuberous plants in all sorts of attractive blotched and mottled variations, which enjoy the warmth and shade of a patio or can be bedded out.

Abutilon, so-called flowering maple although it is not related to the tree, is a fast-growing foliage plant that can impart a woodland air to a walled city garden. The plant should be kept in a sheltered spot out of the wind so that its hollyhocklike flowers will not be blown off. Some varieties have interesting speckled leaves. *Abutilon* grows like a shrub, and a potted specimen is large and unwieldly when brought indoors; to make it easier to manage, train it as a standard (a globe of growth atop a single trunk or stem).

No patio should be without hanging baskets full of foliage and flowering annuals in summer. Pendant tuberous begonias look lovely hanging in humid semi-shade, along with vinca vines, trailing coleus, fragrant-leaved ivy and fancy-leaved geraniums (*Pelargonium* species). Along with their familiar flowers, pelargoniums have the reliably best foliage among the summer plants. The many varieties of pale-margined and blotched leaves in elegant shapes make them favorites for pots and plantings.

Whether you're aiming for a dazzling new display or digging in old friends, foliage annuals are essential

ANNUAL HERBS OF THE FIELD

Find a Home in the Garden

BY CAROLE SAVILLE

A m a r a n t h u s   g a n g e t i c u s

A number of useful herbs growing in fields and wayside places are edible ornamental or fragrant and deserve a place in the home garden. In many cases, the *mauvaise herbe* (French for weed) is really a "good" herb. Some have gone so far as to call the edible ones "designer weeds," and savvy specialty produce farmers are marketing these "new" herbs to creative chefs across the

CAROLE SAVILLE *is a food and garden writer as well as an herb garden design consultant. She lives and gardens in Los Angeles, California.*

country. Improved varieties of wild plants, long treasured in many cultures for their unique flavor and nutritional value, are appearing on dinner plates and in garden catalogs.

Wild mustard (*Brassica nigra*), paints the California hills brilliant yellow in spring, contributing to its name, the Golden State. While driving recently atop the hills overlooking Los Angeles on scenic Mullholland Drive, I was asked abruptly by my passenger, a Sicilian chef, to stop the car. Pointing excitedly to the acid-yellow wild mustard abundantly dotting the landscape, he exclaimed, "*Bruscandoli* — how

Left: Nasturtiums add a peppery taste to salads. Both flowers and leaves are edible.

it reminds me of the hills of Sicily!" Later that week while dining at his restaurant, I was amused by the appearance of several new dishes on the menu: bruscandoli served as a vegetable, sauteed simply with garlic and extra virgin olive oil; bruscandoli risotto (his homage to Northern Italy) and pasta bruscandoli, with a sauce of wild mustard and tomatoes.

B. nigra, one of 80 species of the mustard family, Cruciferae, is the most widespread and is the chief source of mustard, made from the plant's plentiful supply of golden spherical seeds. (Like many so-called weeds, it manufactures a tremendous quantity of seed to ensure widespread growth.) Although mustard (*Brassica hirta* var. *alba*) contains considerably fewer seeds, which are white, the plant's young leaves impart a delicious, hot and spicy pick-up to spring salads.

One of the prettiest wild additions to a spring salad is the nasturtium, another peppery-tasting field herb. The beautiful edible blossoms taste similar to the leaves but slightly more delicate; served with a drop of honey, they are a bonus. Red-orange or yellow are the colors normally associated with nasturtiums, but there are many more. Last fall, while visiting the Orcas Islands, I collected seeds from wild nasturtiums with flowers of dark mahogany, yellow streaked with carmine, orange streaked with vanilla and a deep burgundy — which are now growing in my California garden.

Garden nasturtium (*Tropaeolum majus*), also known as Indian cress, an annual native to South America that has been cultivated in Europe since the late seventeenth century, is a somewhat succulent climber or vigorous spreader. Another climber from Andean South America growing in my garden is *T. tuberosum*, with rounded, lobed leaves, grown for its edible tubers. Traditionally, the tubers are frozen after boiling, or are partially dried, to make the taste more

agreeable. This obviously requires some experimentation. This species, grown as a cool-temperature annual, thrives in a sunny location. My favorite cultivated varieties of nasturtium, readily available in garden catalogs, include: creamy, variegated-leafed 'Alaska', with salmon, golden or orange flowers; 'Empress of India', an heirloom with blue-green leaves and rich vermilion-red flowers; and the free-flowering, spurless 'Whirlybird' (all the other nasturtiums have spurs on the blossoms) with its semidouble blooms. These will grow in sun or shade in hot areas. Finally, the trailing 'Gleam' series, with double and semidouble, multicolored, fragrant flowers, is a knockout for summer hanging baskets in full sun.

Another succulentlike plant excellent in the salad bowl is purslane (*Portulaca oleracea*). It is generally considered a weedy troublemaker, and is routinely rooted out of lawns and gardens. Too bad. Its succulent, rounded leaves and stems add texture and tart flavor to a salad, and are a perfect addition to an herbal mesclun. Originally a native of India, it was brought to our shores from Europe, where its wild form has been grown for centuries. Several cultivated forms are readily available in seed catalogs. Golden purslane (*P. oleracea* var. *sativa*), a variety with large golden leaves and orange-gold stems, is stunning in a salad of mixed green and red lettuces. The cultivated green variety is less striking, but has a slightly better taste and is more vigorous than the golden. Purslane is also a pot herb used both in French cookery (known as *pourpier*), and in Mexican cookery, (known as *verdolagas*).

"Star of the Earth" is the way seventeenth century herbalist Nicholas Culpeper described the lovely salad plants *Plantago coronopus* and *P. verticillata*. The basal leaves resemble a green star. Its Italian name, *herba stella*, is much prettier than buck's horn plantain, its English moniker.

Decorative as well as culinary, the vivid blue, cucumber-scented flowers of borage can be sprinkled over salads of creamy Belgian endive or floated in glasses of lemonade, wine or tonic.

Culpeper may have thought it looked like a star, but it most closely resembles deer horns or antlers. This delicious, toothy herb is eaten raw with mixed greens.

Another star herb, *Stellaria media*, meaning "starry plant of intermediate size" and commonly known as chickweed, was named in Medieval times after its white, star-shaped flowers. You will have to share this one with the birds, as it is one of their favorites. You should have no trouble finding it because it grows abundantly throughout the U.S., as well as in Europe and central and Southern Asia. In Japan it is known as *hakobe*, one the seven herbs of spring. It pushes up through the cold earth in January and its leaves are traditionally chopped and added to a thin rice porridge.

My favorite star-flowered herb is borage (*Borago officinalis*) with its vivid-blue flowers, black anthers and foam-green, fuzzy leaves. To show how long this herb has been around, its name may be derived from a Celtic word referring to courage, which is what it will take to eat its hairy leaves as many herbals, old and new, sug-

gest. I use its lovely cucumber-scented flowers in everything I can think of: sprinkled over salads of creamy Belgian endive; in glasses of lemonade, or with tonic and something stronger at the end of the day; floating in white or red wine; or candied like violets to decorate chocolate pastries. Decorative as well as culinary, borage looks beautiful planted on a ledge or in a situation higher than ground level, where its drooping flowers are more noticeable. The herb is native to the Mediterranean region, and it grows wild in the northeastern United States.

The curious herb of fields and woods, claytonia, or miner's lettuce (*Montia perfoliata*), is native to Cuba. Delicate stems with dainty white flowers rise from the center of the tender, fleshy leaves, which are pointed when young and round out as they grow older. It is wonderful eaten raw with other greens and a light vinaigrette, or cooked like spinach.

No spring salad should be without buttery-leafed corn salad (*Valerianella locusta*), which was given the name from its habit of growing wild among rows of corn. Other names include mache, lamb's lettuce and field salad. Naturalized from Europe, this tender, herbal lettuce was also grown in monastery gardens. One of its cultivated varieties, 'Verte de Cambrai', has petite, teardrop-shaped leaves and a deep green color. Another variety is 'A Grosse Graine', with larger leaves. A very French way to prepare a mache salad includes sliced beets, chopped hard-cooked eggs and walnuts, splashed with a walnut oil vinaigrette. A word of advice: plant mache early, as it can take up to three months to reach full size.

Another "lamb" herb, tasty either raw or cooked like spinach, is lamb's-quarters (*Chenopodium album*). Native to Europe and Asia, it is common throughout the United States. It generally grows from three to five feet, but in certain sections of the country can reach ten feet, so it is best to delegate a separate patch for this plant, a powerhouse of vitamins and minerals. Only the young leaves should be used for salads. Let one plant go to seed and you assure a continuous supply. The seeds can also be dried and cooked like oatmeal or ground and mixed with flour for pastries. A European variety I am trying in my garden this year is the six-foot tall 'Magentaspreen'. When young, its leaves have a true magenta center — yet another beautiful addition to our already colorful salad bowl.

The genus *Chenopodium* has many culinary members. Within the last ten years there has been an ongoing campaign to introduce Americans to quinoa (*C. quinoa*). This excellent cereal grain has more protein than any other grain. Marketed as "mother grain of the Incas" and "supergrain of the future," it is native to the Andes Mountains of South America where it was a staple, along with corn and potatoes, of the Inca civilization. An excellent plant for edible landscapes, quinoa is drought tolerant and has beautiful autumn foliage. It grows four to six feet tall, with arrow-shaped leaves that can also be boiled as a vegetable. The grains of the seedhead are used as cereal, but before cooking them, you must wash off the natural coating or the grain will be quite bitter.

Three other members of the chenopodium or goosefoot family deserve mention. Epazote (*C. ambrosioides*), indigenous to Mexico and widely naturalized and cultivated in warm countries, is a strongly aromatic culinary herb with a camphorlike scent. As is the case with cilantro, you either love this herb or hate it. It is used primarily in Mexican cookery and lends a pungent flavor to all kinds of beans, corn and tomato dishes as well as pork.

C. botrys, known by the heavenly common name ambrosia, is grown for its arching, feathery plumes up to two feet tall with a spicy-sweet perfume. It is an excellent plant to fashion into dried scented wreaths.

Salicornia europaea grows near the sea or in salt marshes, where it naturally absorbs saline from its environment, making its foliage full of aromatic juice. It is eaten fresh, steamed or pickled. Known as samphire or glasswort, it is a delicious, fleshy, succulent herb with clawlike leaves. (Another common name is chicken-claws, which it certainly resembles.) The derivation of its other name, glasswort, is from the soda contained in its leaves, which once was extracted to make glass.

The many varieties of amaranth were other highly nutritious herbal vegetable plants of the New World. Amaranth was cultivated as a favorite food and the main grain crop of the Aztecs. A staple in Asian cookery, amaranth is also known as Chinese spinach. It is the main ingredient of callaloo, the classic soup of Caribbean cookery, and in India it is known as *bhaji*. As a bonus, its beauty certainly puts it in the ornamental category. In this country, love-lies-bleeding (*Amaranthus caudatus*), with its long and feathery cerise tassels, has long been planted in ornamental borders. Amaranth's greens contain more iron and calcium than kale, chard or spinach, and its grains are higher in protein than milk and contain lysine, an amino acid absent in wheat, barley and corn. Of the many leafy varieties, a real show-stopper in a salad is Joseph's coat (*A. gangeticus*), with its brilliant red, yellow and green stripes; it can also be cooked as a vegetable.

Mrs. Burns' Famous Lemon Basil (*Ocimum basilicum*) is a fragrant culinary herb which has been reseeding itself for the past 60 years in southwestern New Mexico. Originally grown by the mother of the founder of Native Seed/SEARCH in Tucson, Arizona, the original seed supposedly came from the Canadian Mennonites who were passing through the territory.

Black cumin, black caraway, fennel flower, nutmeg flower and Roman coriander are all names for *Nigella sativa*, which is both an edible and ornamental herb native to Greece, North Africa and northeastern India. It is also cultivated in France and Germany. Its relative, *N. damascena*, or love-in-a-mist, shows up in the flower section of American seed catalogs. Both are easy to grow. The lacy blue, white or pink flowers of *N. sativa* float atop its feathery green foliage. The seeds that follow the flowers are used to flavor curries or sprinkled over breads and pastries. Both species make exquisite dried flowers.

American pennyroyal (*Hedeoma pulegioides*) is native to our shores and should not be confused with English pennyroyal, a sprawling member of the mint family (*Mentha pulegioides*). Also known as squaw mint, *H. pulegioides*, a drought-tolerant, fragrant herb about one foot in height which resembles a small bush basil with minty

Love-lies-bleeding, *Amaranthus caudatus*, also known as Chinese spinach, is a staple in Asian cookery.

overtones and lavender-blue leaves, is used *sparingly* as a tea.

Annual chamomile (*Matricaria recutita*) from Europe and western Asia is naturalized in North America. It grows about two feet tall and is appreciated for its small, daisylike flowers, which make a soothing apple-scented, "good for what ails you" tea. Its lacy foliage and fragrant white blossoms perfume the air on a hot summer day, making it an all-round ornamental, aromatic and culinary herb.

Finally, there is the quintessentially American sunflower (*Helianthus annuus*), which can grow to ten feet. Present in every part of the country but most abundant in the plains, it is the state flower of the Prairie State, Kansas. The beauties shown nodding their golden heads toward the sun in garden catalogs are cultivated varieties of some of the widespread native species. The seeds are used to produce an edible, healthful oil or eaten whole. These we must share with hungry, pecking birds who have a field day with sunflowers — as they do with most herbal weeds of the wild.

ANNUALS FOR SHADE

BY LAUREN SPRINGER

Rehmannia angulata

To say that shady gardens that include annuals often lack of imagination is to put it mildly. Summer after summer, neighborhood after neighborhood, a sea of wax begonias and impatiens is spreading over the continent. Granted, getting beyond this limited plant palette takes a bit of effort; the more unusual shade-loving annuals must be grown from seed because there isn't enough demand for them. However, just as the perennial boom of the past decade has resulted in a dizzying number of new and unusual perennials, soon more annuals suited to shade will be available at nurseries and garden centers across the country.

LAUREN SPRINGER *is the author of* The Undaunted Garden *(Fulcrum, 1993) and writes for the* Denver Post. *She has gardened professionally on both sides of the Atlantic, writes and photographs for many horticultural books and magazines and lives and gardens in northern Colorado.*

Gardeners can create a lush tropical effect in shady gardens with annuals with unusual foliage and richly hued flowers. A different choice of plants will yield an old-fashioned cottage garden. No matter what

Left: *Coleus* x *hybridus* makes a colorful background for masses of impatiens.

Impatiens balfourii, above, is taller and more elegant than the commonly grown *Impatiens walleriana*.

kind of garden you choose, keep in mind that a humus-rich, moisture-retentive soil and shelter from wind is what most shade-loving annuals require, for it is in the leaf litter of temperate and tropical forests of the world that most have their origins.

There are some early-flowering, frost-tolerant annuals that can turn a shaded area into a delicate canvas of color. Most of these annuals reseed themselves, often germinating in the fall and overwintering, and all prefer cooler weather. Old favorites like Johnny-jump-ups (*Viola tricolor*) and mauve- or white-flowered biennial honesty (*Lunaria annua*) have been grown and loved for centuries. The variegated form of

honesty is especially effective in the shade; if grown from seed, it won't show the white stipples and streaks until it is quite sizable, causing more than a few gardeners to believe they have been cheated.

Sky blue forget-me-nots (*Myosotis sylvatica*) mingle beautifully with orange and yellow Welsh poppies (*Meconopsis cambrica*) but require a moist situation. West Coast native butter-and-eggs (*Limnanthes douglasii*) can add a froth of pale yellow and cream flowers in late spring and early summer.

Poor-man's orchid (*Schizanthus pinnatus*) from South America blooms in ethereal sprays of pink, lavender and white. It

The delicate pink flowers of *Begonia* x *semperflorens* contrast nicely with the dark pink leaves.

rivals the intricately patterned flowers of oncidium orchids or the whiskered and spotted faces of some azaleas and alstroemerias. Poor man's orchid isn't as tolerant of cold as the aforementioned annuals, but still performs best in the coolness of a lightly shaded early-summer garden. Its fernlike, fresh green foliage adds to its beauty.

As the summer heats up, annuals of tropical origin come into their own. The foliage of caladiums is so exotic that sparing use is much more effective than massing. The same can be said for *Coleus* x *hybridus*. The pale chartreuse cultivar 'Pineapple' pairs beautifully with lavender-blue flowers such as those of *Browallia speciosa* or the tall, graceful *Ageratum houstonianum* 'Cut Wonder', or the curiously spotted *Torenia fournieri* and *Mimulus* x *hybridus* — but only if there is plenty of green foliage to act as a foil.

Black-eyed Susan vine (*Thunbergia alata*) has cream, yellow or orange flowers and will climb up dark tree trunks or the supports of a shaded pergola or pavilion. For drier shade, try the golden and variegated forms of hops vine (*Humulus japonicus* 'Aureus' and 'Variegatus') to brighten up a somber vertical spot. They are perennial in mild climates and can be quite rampant.

An unusual, double-flowered form of the commonly grown
Impatiens walleriana.

For a low-growing frothy edge to a shaded bed, *Lobelia erinus* is a good subject, in blue, lavender, rose or white. Light shade keeps it in flower much longer than full sun. A favorite of mine, unfortunately much less well known, is blue woodruff (*Asperula orientalis*). It resembles its close relative, perennial sweet woodruff (*Galium odoratum*) in flower and in leaf, yet blooms for a much longer time. The softly fragrant, dainty clusters of pale blue flowers above whorled foliage are a fine addition under large shrubs.

For a more refined, formal look, try an annual groundcover of Madagascar periwinkle (*Catharanthus roseus*). The vinca-like flowers in shades of rose, pink and white, often with a contrasting darker eye, are borne for several months on a rich carpet of glossy, dark-green leaves. This plant can tolerate a variety of soil and moisture conditions.

I have a weakness for annuals that have the grace and proportions of perennials rather than the stout, overly floriferous selections so popular today. In place of the sweeps of *Impatiens walleriana,* I'd like to see more of the taller, elegant *Impatiens balfourii,* with bicolored flowers of mauve and white which do not overpower the plant and mingle much better with perennials and shrubs in a shady garden. Com-

This form of *Coleus blumei* has golden edges that set off
the dark red centers.

bined with a small grouping of polka-dot plant (*Hypoestes phyllostachya*), whose leaves are subtly marked with small pink or white dots, echoing the flower colors of the impatiens, it is as pleasing as any perennial composition.

A similarly soft combination marries the tall, foxglovelike mauve and white flower spires of *Ceratotheca triloba* with fragrant white starbursts of giant woodland tobacco (*Nicotiana sylvestris*). On a smaller scale, rose-flowered, gloxinialike *Rehmannia angulata*, a spreading perennial in areas with mild winters but annual in zones 6 and colder, pairs well with the chartreuse, nodding bells of three-foot

Nicotiana langsdorfii. All the nicotianas, or flowering tobaccos, are wonderful annuals for part shade. The pale green, white and pink forms show up better in the muted light than do the deep red ones. Unfortunately the breeders have dwarfed them and taken away most of their intoxicating perfume, but with the resurging interest in both scented and heirloom plants, the older forms are becoming more available. I hope that this same sentiment will turn shade gardeners away from planting just begonias and impatiens. The flora of this planet is miraculously varied, and there's no reason that our gardens shouldn't reflect this beautiful diversity.

TENDER PERENNIALS

for Annual Excitement

BY JACK POTTER

Salvia 'Purple Majesty'

n established gardens annuals or tender perennials provide splashes of season-long color available from few hardy perennials. (Tender perennials are perennials that aren't hardy in your climate and won't make it through the winter without protection, if at all.) The greatest rewards come from making those splashes of color different from year to year; if you're going to

JACK POTTER, *a writer and photographer, is curator of the Scott Arboretum in Swarthmore, Pennsylvania. He is the author of* Roses *(Time-Life, 1990).*

replant each year, do use the chance for change.

At the Scott Arboretum in Swarthmore, Pennsylvania, we have been using annual plantings to create that sense of change, striving to surprise our visitors with fresh color schemes and new plants. Many of the less-familiar plants in our recent yearly plantings have been tender perennials, from which we take cuttings to winter on a windowsill or in a greenhouse or cold-frame. Our aim is to have displays that can be replicated fairly easily by home gardeners, so we use these plants in small areas (especially containers) within our larger gardens of hardy, permanent plantings.

Left: *Salvia coccinea*, Texas sage, flowers in light shade or sun.

The results are worth the effort. Among our favorite tender perennials in recent years have been salvias, verbenas and agastaches.

Salvias

Salvia guaranitica, anise-scented sage, was our first sage venture beyond the commonly grown red *S. splendens* and blue *S. farinacea*. It grows to three feet in a season and produces a continual, June-to-frost succession of spikes of deep blue, strongly lipped, tubular flowers over rich green, aromatic foliage. 'Argentina Skies' is a cultivar with silvery blue flowers. It blends softly with neighboring gray or silver foliage, and also flatters bright nearby flowers such as orange kniphofias. *Salvia* 'Purple Majesty' is a *S. guaranitica* hybrid with larger, more sprawling growth (it may need staking) and with slightly larger, purple flowers from August to frost. *Salvia guaranitica* 'Late Blooming Giant' is taller still (five to six feet), and is sure to need staking. It bears broader, darker, more violet-hued flowers than the species, but not until October, so it is a gambler's plant here: some years frost comes early enough to prevent bloom. This form is very similar to *S. guaranitica* 'Black and Blue' or Costa Rican blue sage. All the salvias above except *S.* 'Purple Majesty' have lived through winters here in Pennsylvania in protected spots, or through mild winters, or under deep mulch. The plants are somewhat tuberous and will send up new shoots from deep underground, so they tolerate a thick winter mulch without danger of suffoca-

Salvia rutilans, pineapple sage, has deliciously scented leaves and long spikes of brilliant red, tubular flowers in fall.

Verbena tenuisecta, seen here at the front of the border, has lavender-blue flowers and finely dissected foliage.

tion. They prefer full sun or very light shade. These blue salvias are hummingbird favorites, preferred even over the red-tubed flowers of other sages.

Our most exciting red salvia, both in containers and in a red and purple border, has been *S. vanhouttii*. Garnet-colored calyces appear in July, becoming more abundant and opening with brighter, crimson flowers from August through the first light frosts. Growth is loose and graceful to about four feet, as though the common scarlet bedding sage had been stretched out into a lightly branching plant and its flowers repainted in rich and subtle hues. In full sun *S. vanhouttii* stands alone, but in light shade it needs some support.

Salvia miniata prefers light shade over full sun, grows to three feet and has spikes of scarlet flowers. The flower spikes are always loose enough to reveal the striking contrast with the glossy, handsome, bright green foliage. The plant may be hardy in zones 9 to 10 on the U.S.D.A. hardiness zone map.

Salvia coccinea, Texas sage, grows to the same height and also has scarlet flowers. It flowers surprisingly well in light shade as well as full sun. Texas sage self-sows freely in our gardens. Seeds germinate after the soil has warmed, and the plants bloom within six weeks; young plants are much bushier if their tips are pinched once or twice. 'Lady in Red' is a compact-growing 1992 All America Selection, available from seed. A white form and a bicolored white and shrimp-pink form are available as plants or seed (and will breed true from seed if the plants are isolated). The white and pink form (*S. coccinea* 'Bicolor') has filled in bare areas of a silver, pink and lavender mixed border at the Arboretum. It flowers from late June or early July to frost, and it is beautiful in the morning; on sunny days, however, most of its flowers become torn by bees forcing their way down the narrow corolla tubes, leaving the plants looking sparse and bedraggled. Ordinary scarlet forms are amply proportioned and escape damage; we haven't grown the white forms.

Salvia greggii forms and hybrids have

broad-lipped flowers in shades of red, white, rose or salmon (and, most recently, yellow). These are drought-tolerant plants from arid regions; they require sharp soil drainage, and bloom poorly while nights are hot and humid. Their best flowering is likely to come after the first fall frosts — if they can be protected from those frosts. I find them a bit frustrating here.

Salvia chamaedryoides, germander sage, has similar requirements and flowers at about the same time, but its gray foliage, pure sky-blue flowers and more restrained, two-foot stature have made it a better container plant for us. Even a few flowers of such extraordinary blue give pleasure.

Salvia rutilans, pineapple sage, and *Salvia elegans*, honey melon sage, resemble each other closely: three and a half-foot bushy plants with deliciously scented foliage and long spikes of brilliant red tubular flowers. In the fall there is a race to see which comes first, *S. rutilans* blooms or the first frost; the salvia loses in some years. We have just acquired *S. elegans*, which starts flowering in midsummer and carries on until frost.

Salvia leucantha, Mexican bush sage, is another late-season gambler's plant. Plants grow to four and a half feet. The undersides of the leaves and the stems are white and fuzzy, so the overall foliage effect is softly gray-green. Calyces are also fuzzy, and reddish purple, with flowers either in matching purple or white. Plants in bloom look like late, narrow-spiked and elegant buddleias.

Salvia involucrata, rosebud sage, may also wait until October to bloom. We grow a form from Wave Hill, the public garden in the Bronx, and one from Richard Dufresne, the North Carolina salviaphile. The latter begins to flower in July, is bushier and blooms more prolifically through the fall than the former. Its rose-pink flowers appear over broad green leaves with pinkish veins and petioles. Full sun produces the strongest plants and heaviest flowering for *S. rutilans*, *S. leucantha* and *S. involucrata* here at Scott Arboretum.

Verbenas

Most seed-grown bedding verbenas stop blooming during the heat of summer. A number of species and hybrids we have recently grown, however, thrive on our summer heat and humidity, and some bloom heavily through fall as well. These are all low plants of 15 inches or less that creep or run, rooting where leaf nodes on the stems touch the soil (a clue that propagation from cuttings is quick and easy). Individual flowers are flat and small, half an inch or less, but grouped in showy, dome-shaped clusters that continue to elongate

The spectacular flower spike of pineapple sage seen close up.

Salvia guaranitica, anise-scented sage, produces continual June-to-frost spikes of deep blue flowers.

and form new buds. They go on flowering well for us even when spent flower clusters are left on the plants.

Verbena 'Sissinghurst' has slightly incised foliage almost hidden by bright pink flowers with enough tones of both salmon and magenta to work well in color schemes headed in either direction. It is our best herbaceous butterfly plant, and such a favorite that we have repeatedly used it, with gray and blue companions, in our most prominent pots. Containers provide the needed good drainage but demand faithful watering and periodic applications of fertilizer.

Verbena canadensis has forms and hybrids in mauve, pink, purple, white and red. The heaviest blooming for us, over the longest season, has been a red-violet form from Montrose Nursery with no cultivar name. We have massed it in a border of deep pink 'Carefree Beauty' roses, and both plants have flowered from June until well after frost. It was a mainstay in our red and purple border, and also a great companion to the gray-white, long-blooming

hardy perennial *Calamintha nepeta*, joined in September by mauve-pink colchicums. In our highest voltage containers this verbena was paired with the vivid orange annual *Zinnia linearis*. For us, some *V. canadensis* plants survive some winters. (Through the mild 1990-1991 winter all the plants in raised beds in my home roof-deck garden remained nearly evergreen and began to bloom again in April.) A clear red *V. canadensis* hybrid (also from Montrose Nursery) and the pale pink *V.* 'Appleblossom' have been superb container plants at Scott; this year the red, as true and clear a primary color as I have ever seen in a flower, takes its first turn in open ground.

Verbena peruviana, with scarlet flowers, and *Verbena tenera* var. *maonettii*, with magenta flowers edged white, are both creeping plants that grow four or five inches high but spread at least a couple of feet in a season. These tight mats can make a snug home for spider mites; *V. peruviana* was a little disappointing in our red and purple border.

Verbena tenuisecta is medium in height,

to about twelve inches, with thin stems and finely dissected foliage. Flowers in the typical form are lavender-blue, white in the cultivar 'Alba'. These may self-sow here, and are hardy in zones 8-10. Lavender-blue *V. tenuisecta*, with its soft color and lacy foliage, was an even prettier companion than the red-violet *V. canadensis* for deep pink roses, but bloomed most profusely in early summer and declined sharply after August. Two new hybrids from Edith Eddleman's borders at North Carolina State University Arboretum maintain the delicate foliage texture, add new flower colors and have been among the most abundant, longest, latest-blooming plants in our gardens. *Verbena* 'Edith', with soft mauve flowers and slightly more compact habit, bloomed past hard frosts and almost up to

Christmas last year. *Verbena* 'Flamingo Border Pink' is taller than 'Edith', bears bright magenta-pink flowers and is about as floriferous.

All these verbenas perform best with well-drained soil and full sun; the *Verbena tenuisecta* group is more tolerant than the others of very light shade.

Agastaches

Agastaches, or hyssops, are related to salvias and have spikes of small, tubular flowers. *Agastache* 'Firebird' may grow to four feet where it is hardy; plants in their first season from cuttings will reach about half that height, perhaps distracted from growth by their continually increasing bloom from June to late fall. Flowers are narrow tubes about an inch long, opening

Salvia 'Purple Majesty' is a large, sprawling plant that may need to be staked.

JACK POTTER

JACK POTTER

The tubular flowers of *Agastache* 'Firebird' open orange and turn magenta, for a smoky, burnt-orange effect.

softer colors.

Adding a few tender perennials to a garden doesn't require a large greenhouse or a Victorian estate staff. Plants of borderline hardiness will winter securely in a cold-frame. Many tender plants grow large in a single season, so small numbers of plants have disproportionate impact. Some of the salvias (especially *S. leucantha* and *S. involucrata*) quickly become shrubby plants with strong presence. The vigorous, carpeting verbenas cover large areas or weave into their neighbors. Softwood cuttings taken early in fall, before cold weather, usually root easily (for agastache cuttings, use basal, non-flowering shoots). Even a few plants overwintered on a windowsill — or purchased in late spring — can make a big difference in a garden.

orange and becoming magenta, borne in loose but abundant spikes. The overall effect is a subtle, smoky burnt-orange, very beautiful beside the purple foliage of 'Crimson Pygmy' barberries, and the chief inspiration for a planned burnt-orange and amber border. *A.* 'Firebird' to me resembles a penstemon; it has the air of a plant for full sun, but one end of our barberry bed is shaded much of the day in autumn and the plants there performed almost as well as the others.

We acquired *A.* 'Firebird' from Stonecrop, in New York's cold Hudson Valley, with a strong recommendation but no expectation that it would be winter hardy. We have since heard that it has consistently overwintered in Massachusetts. Richard Dufresne, who hybridized this and a number of other agastaches, rates it as hardy in zone 6. This past winter has been too mild to pose a real test, but our plants so far look fine.

We are growing cuttings of other agastaches, some perhaps hardy here, others almost certainly not. 'Apricot Sunrise' will join our amber and orange scheme; 'Pink Panther' and 'Pink Lemonade' will support

Sources

Canyon Creek Nursery
3527 Dry Creek Rd.
Oroville, CA 95965
(916) 533-2166

Glasshouse Works Greenhouse
Church Street, P.O. Box 97
Stewart, OH 45778-0097
(614) 662-2142

Logee's Greenhouses
141 North Street
Danielson, CT 06239
(203) 774-8038

Montrose Nursery
P.O. Box 957
Hillsborough, NC 27278
(919) 732-7778

The Sandy Mush Herb Nursery
Route 2, Surrett Cove Road
Leicester, NC 28748
(704) 683-2014

ANNUALS
FOR THE CONTAINER GARDEN

BY TOM PEACE

Gloriosa rothschildiana

There is nothing quite as elegant as an outdoor summer retreat adorned with pots overflowing with exquisite foliage and colorful flowers. A rustic whiskey barrel filled with jewel-toned dahlias, cannas and zinnias set among burgundy-leafed castor bean and purple fountain grass warms up a sunny deck, while a classic urn displaying coleus, tuberous begonias and delicate curtains of trailing lobelia highlights the shaded terrace.

Container plantings add style and life to any outdoor living space. The key to success is finding the right plants to satisfy both the cultural and aesthetic requirements dictated by each site. Some plants need to remain cool in order to perform throughout the summer months, while some like it hot. It is important to investigate the prospective growing space before spending your time and money on the wrong plants.

One particularly lovely combination for a cool north-facing patio (with the pots kept right up against the shady building away

TOM PEACE, *a garden designer, writer and nurseryman, makes use of a wide variety of plants to create gardens in Arizona, Colorado and Texas.*

Left: Containers of nasturtiums, petunias, lobelia and alyssum cascade down the stairs.

from hot sun) includes the old-fashioned standard fuchsia (*Fuchsia* x *hybrida*) with red sepals and violet corolla, and the red tuberous begonia (*Begonia* x *hybrida*), in a mass of white or hot-pink impatiens and purple swan river daisy (*Brachycome iberidifolia*), accented with a solitary polka dot plant (*Hypoestes phyllostachya*). This combination can be assembled in one container or an assortment of smaller, different-sized pots, each highlighting a particular component of the grouping. In a spot that absolutely bakes in the summer sun, try the purple princess flower (*Tibouchina urvilleana*) with lemon-yellow lantana (*Lantana camara*) and brilliant ruby-red verbena (*Verbena* x *hybrida*) cascading over the edge of a dark slate planter.

Instead of a combination of plants, you may want to mass one species or cultivar. Moss rose (*Portulaca* species), periwinkle (*Catharanthus roseus*), *Gazania rigens* and verbena can easily hold their own in the face of heat and drought. Begonias, impatiens or violas can brighten up dark balconies and patios with beautiful blossoms.

I would not want to lead you to believe that only blooming plants can grace container gardens; foliage is as overlooked in pots as it is in the ground. When I design plantings, I usually consider the flowers secondary to the leaf forms of the plants I combine. There are three types of foliage: bold, linear and fine-textured. Just as they do in

Here, sunny marigolds and dahlias are massed in clay pots. The tiny purple trailing flower is lobelia.

Helichrysum petiolare and
Tradescantia pallida, an unusual and
elegant combination.

the garden, foliage plants define and anchor container plantings. For the shady corner, imagine an old kettle brimming with white *Caladium* x *hortulanum*, variegated spider plant (*Chlorophytum comosum* 'Variegatum') and *Asparagus densiflorus* 'Sprengeri'. This *menage a trois* is a knockout in virtually every climate of the U.S.

A large terra cotta pot with red-leafed castor bean (*Ricinus communis*), dusty miller and purple heart (*Tradescantia pallida*) can easily dominate a patio in the hot sun or anchor additional containers featuring orange and yellow flowers.

Container gardens have much in common with cut-flower arrangements inasmuch as they present a distinctly framed assortment of colors and textures. Adventurous designers create lovely mixed "bouquets" by unabashedly mixing temperates and tropicals, elegant flowers and weeds.

When shopping for plants don't limit yourself to the overused annuals offered by local garden centers. Explore their hothous-

es and outdoor perennial collections for new and different textures, colors and architectural forms. Try using species and forms of *Eucalyptus*, *Agave*, variegated *Ficus* or *Dracaena marginata* 'Tricolor' to embellish displays in the sun, and *Sansevieria*, *Pothos*, rex begonias or a myriad of tropical ferns in shady arrangements. Blue fescue (*Festuca ovina* 'Glauca'), Japanese blood grass (*Imperata cylindrica* 'Rubra'), pink fountain grass (*Pennisetum alopecuroides*) or gardener's garters (*Phalaris arundinacea*) are among the grasses whose linear foliage can be a welcome addition to your pots.

Hostas in shades of emerald, blue and gold, *Bergenia cordifolia* and *Ligularia dentata* are three good examples of hardy perennials that add bold foliage to combinations in shaded settings. For sunnier positions, try silver clary (*Salvia argentea*) and silver mullein (*Verbascum bombyciferum*), both stunning with *Heuchera* 'Palace Purple' or, for a unique touch, garden rhubarb.

Don't ignore summer bulbs for accent in container combinations. My favorites include summer callas, especially yellow *Zantedeschia elliottiana* and white *Z. albo-maculata*. Both feature distinctly spotted, arrowhead-shaped foliage and add a wonderful touch to the shaded corner. Another choice bulb is *Achimenes*, which gives a nonstop performance of pink, white or purple blooms when kept warm enough. Gloriosa lily (*G. rothschildiana*) can be added to a large grouping (for it does grow tall and needs other plants for support) and makes a sensational accent with bronze-leaf canna 'Cheyenne', blue mealy sage (*Salvia farinacea*), yellow hibiscus (*H. rosa-sinensis*), nasturtiums and purple basil (*Ocimum basilicum* 'Purple Ruffles'). Like *Achimenes*, the South African chincherinchee (*Ornithogalum thyrsoides*) can be grown on its own and makes a wonderful centerpiece for the summer table. Indeed, the bulbs can be tucked into almost any container arrangement as their white flowers and simple foliage harmonize with just about everything.

Some annuals and tender perennials absolutely must be tried despite the fact that searching for them is a little like the quest for the Holy Grail. Most are easy to grow, notwithstanding their rarity, and can be used in a wide variety of sites. Woodland tobacco (*Nicotiana sylvestris*) is a garden giant that stays smaller in containers but retains its bold stature and striking interest. Its large, vibrant leaves are whorled up the pyramidal plant, terminating in an explosion of pendant, white tubular flowers that are deliciously fragrant on summer evenings. Woodland tobacco makes an excellent focus for a pastel collection, or an all-white garden in a white terra cotta pot. I like it best towering above plants that contrast with its spring-green foliage, such as Chinese basil (*Perilla frutescens*), dark red coleus and burgundy fountain grass, enlivened further by jewel-tone nasturtiums and marigold 'Lemon Gem'.

Another great performer is *Fuchsia* 'Gartenmeister'. It is versatile as a soloist. I use mine, a six-year-old shrub in a five-gallon pot, to temporarily fill blank spots in the garden as well as accent collections of other potted flowers. 'Gartenmeister' can play a part in a trio or quintet, with its clusters of coral-orange trumpet flowers dancing above *Nicotiana alata* 'Nicki Lime' and blue trailing lobelia (*L. erinus*), perhaps with yel-

Old stumps showcase dahlias, ivy geranium, pansies and lobelia.

Dusty miller sets off pink ivy
geraniums and impatiens.
Chrysanthemums bloom in the bed.

low coleus and Japanese blood grass.

Somewhat harder to find but worth the effort (even if you have to order it by mail) is *Helichrysum petiolare* 'Limelight'. The plant is a bit particular about its needs (full sun and good drainage) but the chartreuse foliage glows. Fortunately, 'Limelight' looks splendid on its own in a pot or with ivy geraniums (*Pelargonium peltatum*), which can live with its restrictive cultural requirements. The species *H. petiolare*, I might add, has the same full form but is a cool silvery color, making it a substitute for dusty miller.

New to me last year but already one of my favorites is fan flower (*Scaevola aemula* 'Blue Wonder') whose sprawling stems are terminated by endlessly blooming fans of blue flowers resembling those of lobelia. The plant combines well with yellow coleus, pink flowering tobacco or 'Gartenmeister'.

Two other candidates for adding a touch of blue to container gardens are *Ageratum* 'Cut Wonder' and tall verbena (*Verbena bonariensis*). Both plants are somewhat leggy and therefore a bit awkward on their own but look just fine in a crowd. 'Cut Wonder' mixes well with most everything and doesn't get as much dead flower accumulation as many of the other ageratums. It is smashing in sun or partial shade with rose-pink geraniums and yellow *Chrysanthemum multicaule*. Tall verbena is quite a bit taller and needs to be grown in a big pot for best results, combined with other heat lovers such as orange Mexican fire bush (*Hamelia patens*) or scarlet *Salvia coccinea* and yellow gloriosa daisy (*Rudbeckia hirta*) to balance the spectrum.

Just about any plant that combines well in a mixed border will do well in a container, provided that it is large enough (the larger plants will need a pot 15 inches minimum in diameter). Annuals like castor bean, spider flower (*Cleome hassleriana*), Mexican sunflower (*Tithonia rotundifolia*), woodland tobacco, canna and dahlias all require spacious accommodations. So do nasturtiums and California poppies, even though they do not attain the same giant proportions. Large pots lend themselves to more diverse plantings and do not need to be watered as frequently during hot, dry weather. Unless you are inclined to spend your summer with the hose or watering can in hand, do not plant in any pot smaller than eight inches in diameter.

The one drawback to very large planters is that it may take your entire garden budget just to fill them with soil, at which point you will never be able to move them again. There is a simple solution. As only about 15 to 18 inches of soil is needed for rooting, fill the bottom of a deep planter with anything organic or inorganic that is lightweight and inexpensive — bark mulch, pine cones or styrofoam packing peanuts — and then place the soil mix on top. This allows you to spend your money on what counts — the plants. Furthermore, you won't need an army to help move your containers should the desire to redecorate strike you in midseason.

The best choice for containers is still the classic terra cotta pot, available in a myriad of sizes and shapes and even buff and white. Naturally porous, the clay pot allows the soil to breathe and cool the root zone via evaporation. While this is a boon for plants that need good drainage, it makes retaining moisture for water-loving plants more difficult. An easy remedy is to paint the inside of smaller pots and those for moist soils with the black tar paint sold for coating cut tree limbs. It is sold as an easy-to-apply spray; be careful to stay two or three inches below the rim to hide the black lining below soil level.

Of course, many other types of containers are available, from wood, metal and plastic to antique household objects. Anything goes — both in your choice of containers and your selection of annuals. ✿

Salvia farinacea with its tall bluish spikes, pink *Verbena rigida* and trailing *Vinca* grace this decorative urn.

ANNUALS

FOR SPECIAL PURPOSES

FOR FRAGRANCE

Gaillardia

Pelargonium

Abronia spp.	Sand verbenas
Agastache spp.	Agastaches
Ageratum houstonianum	Ageratum
Anethum graveolens	Dill
Angelica archangelica	Angelica
Asperula orientalis	Blue woodruff
Calendula officinalis	Pot marigold
Centaurea moschata 'Imperialis'	Sweet sultan
Cheiranthus cheiri	Wallflower
Coriandrum sativum	Coriander
Datura inoxia	Angel's trumpet
Dianthus barbatus	Sweet William
D. chinensis	Pink
Erysimum hieraciifolium	Siberian wallflower
Eschscholzia californica	California poppy
Foeniculum vulgare	Fennel
Hedysarum coronarium	French honeysuckle
Heliotropium arborescens	Cherry pie
Hesperis matronalis	Sweet rocket
Iberis spp.	Candytufts
Ipomoea alba	Moon vine

continued on the next page

Night-scented stock

Pelargonium graveolens

Purple verbena

continued from the prior page

Ipomopsis aggregata	Skyrocket
Lantana camara	Lantana
Lathyrus odoratus	Sweet pea
Lobularia maritima	Sweet alyssum
Lunaria annua	Honesty
Malcolmia maritima	Virginia stock
Matricaria recutita	German chamomile
Matthiola longipetala ssp. *bicornis*	Stock
M. incana	Evening stock
Mentzelia lindleyi	Blazing star
Mirabilis jalapa	Four-o'clock
Monarda citriodora	Lemon balm
Myosotis sylvatica	Forget-me-not
Nemophila menziesii	Baby blue eyes
Nicotiana spp.	Flowering tobaccos
Ocimum basilicum	Basil
Oenothera spp.	Evening primroses
Pelargonium spp.	Geraniums
Petroselinum crispum	Parsley
Petunia x *hybrida*	Petunia
Phlox drummondii	Annual phlox
Reseda odorata	Mignonette
Salvia spp.	Sages
Tagetes spp.	Marigolds
Tanacetum parthenium	Feverfew
Trachymene coerulea	Blue lace flower
Tropaeolum majus	Nasturtium
Verbena x *hybrida*	Verbena

Cup and saucer vine

Morning glories

Lobelia erinus

t = trailing		c = climbing
Begonia spp.	t	Begonias, some types
Browallia speciosa	t	Browallia
Catharanthus roseus	t	Madagascar periwinkle
Clitoria spp.	c	Butterfly peas
Cobaea scandens	c	Cup and saucer vine
Cucurbita spp.	c,t	Gourd vines
Dolichos lablab	c	Hyacinth bean
Eccremocarpus sp.	c	Sunset creeper
Fuchsia spp.	t	Fuchsias
Humulus japonicus	c,t	Hop vine
Ipomoea purpurea	c,t	Morning glory
Ipomoea quamoclit	c	Cypress vine
Lantana spp.	t	Lantanas
Lathyrus odoratus	c	Sweet pea
Lobelia erinus	t	Lobelia
Merremia spp.	c	Wood roses
Pelargonium peltatum	c	Ivy geranium
Petunia x *hybrida*	t	Petunias, some types
Phaseolus coccineus	c	Scarlet runner bean
Plumbago spp.	c,t	Plumbagos
Portulaca spp.	t	Portulacas, some types
Rhodochiton atrosanguineum	t	Purple bell vine
Sanvitalia procumbens	t	Creeping zinnia
Thunbergia alata	c,t	Black-eyed Susan vine
Tropaeolum majus	c,t	Nasturtiums, some types
T. peregrinum	c	Canary creeper
Verbena spp.	t	Verbenas, some types
Vinca major, V. minor	t	Vincas
Zinnia angustifolia	t	Narrow-leaved zinnia

Globe amaranth

Celosia cristata	Cock's comb, plume flower
Gomphrena globosa	Globe amaranth
Helichrysum bracteatum	Strawflower
Limonium sinuatum	Statice
Physalis alkekengi	Chinese lantern
Xeranthemum annuum	Immortelle

FOR BIRDS & BUTTERFLIES

Cosmos bipinnatus

Helianthus annuus

b = butterflies

s = songbirds (they eat the seeds so don't deadhead)

h = hummingbirds (attracted to red, tubular flowers)

m = moths

Ageratum houstonianum	**b**	Floss flower
Antirrhinum majus	**h**	Snapdragon
Callistephus chinensis	**b,s**	China aster
Coreopsis tinctoria	**b,s**	Tickseed
Cosmos bipinnatus	**b,s**	Cosmos
Dianthus spp.	**b**	Pinks
Echium lycopsis	**b**	Viper's bugloss
Fuchsia x *hybrida*	**h**	Fuchsia
Gaillardia pulchella	**b**	Annual Indian blanket
Helianthus annuus	**b,s**	Sunflower
Heliotropium arborescens	**b**	Cherry pie

Statice

Tropaeolum majus

Zinnia elegans

Impatiens walleriana	**b,s**	Busy Lizzie
Ipomoea alba	**b,m**	Moon vine
I. purpurea	**b**	Morning glory
Lantana spp.	**b**	Lantanas
Limonium sinuatum	**b**	Statice
Lobelia erinus	**b**	Lobelia
Lobularia maritima	**b**	Sweet alyssum
Mirabilis jalapa	**b,m**	Four o'clock
Myosotis sylvatica	**s**	Forget-me-not
Nicotiana alata	**b,h**	Jasmine tobacco (moths)
Pelargonium spp.	**h**	Geraniums
Petunia x *hybrida*	**h**	Petunias
Phlox drummondii	**b,h**	Drummond's phlox
Portulaca grandiflora	**s**	Moss rose
Reseda odorata	**b**	Mignonette
Salvia splendens	**h**	Scarlet sage
Scabiosa atropurpurea	**b**	Pincushion flower
Tagetes spp.	**b,s**	Marigolds
Tithonia rotundifolia	**b,s**	Mexican sunflower
Tropaeolum majus	**b,h**	Nasturtium
Verbena bonariensis	**b**	Tall verbena
Zinnia elegans	**b,s**	Zinnia

Cleome hassleriana

California poppy

Petunia

Argemone platyceras	Prickly poppy
Brachycome iberidifolia	Swan River daisy
Centaurea cyanus	Bachelor button
Cleome hassleriana	Spider flower
Coreopsis tinctoria	Tickseed
Cosmos bipinnatus	Cosmos
Cuphea ignea	Firecracker plant
Dianthus spp.	Pinks
Dimorphotheca sp.	Cape marigold
Daucus carota	Queen Anne's lace (biennial)
Diascia spp.	Twinspurs
Dorotheanthus	Livingstone daisy
Dyssodia tenuiloba	Dahlberg daisy
Emilia javanica	Tassel flower
Eschscholzia californica	California poppy
Euphorbia marginata	Snow-on-the-mountain
Gaillardia pulchella	Annual Indian blanket
Gazania rigens	Treasure flower
Gomphrena globosa	Globe amaranth
Gypsophila elegans	Sunflower
Helipterum spp.	Strawflowers
Hunnemannia fumariifolia	Mexican poppy

Dusty miller

Verbena tenuisecta

Xeranthemum annuum

Ipomoea purpurea	Morning glory
Lavatera trimestris	Rose mallow
Kochia scoparia	Burning bush
Limonium sinuatum	Statice
Linum grandiflorum	Scarlet flax
Linaria spp.	Baby snaps
Mentzelia lindleyi	Blazing star
Mesembryanthemum spp.	Ice plants
Mirabilis jalapa	Four o'clock,
Nolana spp.	Chilean bellflowers
Oenothera biennis	Evening primrose
Papaver somniferum	Opium poppy
Perilla frutescens	Perilla
Portulaca grandiflora	Moss rose
Rudbeckia hirta	Black-eyed Susan
Senecio cineraria	Dusty miller
Silene armeria	Pink catchfly
Tropaeolum majus	Nasturtium
Venidium spp.	Cape daisies
Verbascum spp.	Mullein (biennial)
Verbena spp.	Verbenas
Xeranthemum annuum	Immortelle

MAP

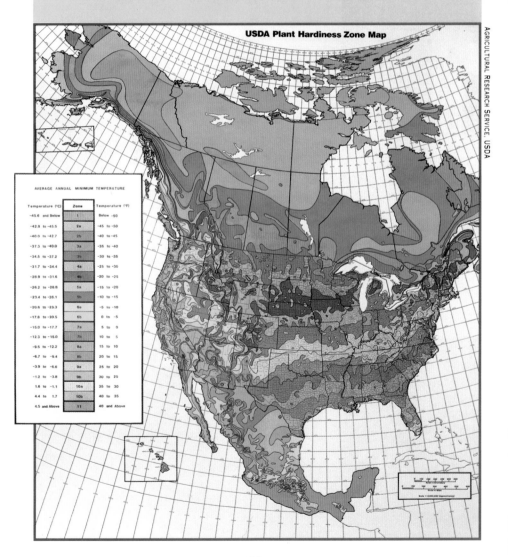

USDA Plant Hardiness Zone Map

AGRICULTURAL RESEARCH SERVICE, USDA

AVERAGE ANNUAL MINIMUM TEMPERATURE

Temperature (°C)	Zone	Temperature (°F)
-45.6 and Below	1	Below -50
-42.8 to -45.5	2a	-45 to -50
-40.0 to -42.7	2b	-40 to -45
-37.3 to -40.0	3a	-35 to -40
-34.5 to -37.2	3b	-30 to -35
-31.7 to -34.4	4a	-25 to -30
-28.9 to -31.6	4b	-20 to -25
-26.2 to -28.8	5a	-15 to -20
-23.4 to -26.1	5b	-10 to -15
-20.6 to -23.3	6a	-5 to -10
-17.8 to -20.5	6b	0 to -5
-15.0 to -17.7	7a	5 to 0
-12.3 to -15.0	7b	10 to 5
-9.5 to -12.2	8a	15 to 10
-6.7 to -9.4	8b	20 to 15
-3.9 to -6.6	9a	25 to 20
-1.2 to -3.8	9b	30 to 25
1.6 to -1.1	10a	35 to 30
4.4 to 1.7	10b	40 to 35
4.5 and Above	11	40 and Above

INDEX
BY COMMON NAME